MW01088236

AMERICAN NARCISSISM:

The Myth of National Superiority

AMERICAN NARCISSISM:

The Myth of National Superiority

Wilber W. Caldwell

Algora Publishing
New York

© 2006 by Algora Publishing.
All Rights Reserved
www.algora.com

No portion of this book (beyond what is permitted by
Sections 107 or 108 of the United States Copyright Act of 1976)
may be reproduced by any process, stored in a retrieval system,
or transmitted in any form, or by any means, without the
express written permission of the publisher.
ISBN-13: 978-0-87586-467-9 (trade paper)
ISBN-13: 978-0-87586-468-6 (hard cover: alk. paper)
ISBN-13: 978-0-87586-469-3 (ebook)

Library of Congress Cataloging-in-Publication Data —

Caldwell, Wilber W.
    American narcissism: the myth of national superiority / Wilber W. Caldwell.
        p. cm.
    Includes bibliographical references and index.
    ISBN-13: 978-0-87586-467-9 (trade paper: alk. paper)
    ISBN-13: 978-0-87586-468-6 (hard cover: alk. paper)
    ISBN-13: 978-0-87586-469-3 (ebook)
    1. National characteristics, American. 2. Nationalism—United States. 3.
Narcissism—Political aspects—United States. 4. Political culture—United States.
5. Imperialism. 6. United States—Territorial expansion. 7. United States—Foreign
relations. I. Title.

    E169.1.C19 2006
    305.800973—dc22

                        2006022779

Front Cover: Businessman Gazing into Laptop Mirror
Image: © Images.com/Corbis
Creator Name: Herve Baudry

Printed in the United States

Acknowledgement

As always, I wish to express my loving gratitude to Mary Fitzhugh Parra for devotion, tea, sympathy, and for her enduring patience in the face of my endless ponderings.

TABLE OF CONTENTS

PREFACE

*It would be futile to attempt to convince a North American,
although the contribution his nation has made to the evolution of liberty and utility has undoubtedly been substantial,
and should rightfully qualify as a universal contribution,
indeed, as a contribution to humanity, it is not so great as to
cause the axis of the world to shift...*[1]
José Enrique Rodó in Ariel, 1900.

Ariel, the extraordinary work of Uruguayan author José Enrique Rodó,
remains virtually unknown in the United States, but over a hundred years after
its publication it is still widely read and quoted in Latin America. It is a book of
seemingly timeless insight. Rodó's generous turn-of-the-century praise of the
best qualities of the United States still accurately describes our national
strengths today. Likewise, his descriptions of our national self-congratulatory
arrogance and blind evangelical nationalism remain every bit as apt at the
beginning of the 21st century as they were a hundred years ago. While in one
breath Rodó praises US ingenuity, in the next he wonders why we don't simply
presume to rewrite the Holy Bible, inserting ourselves on the very first page.

The sad fact is that the America of today is even more arrogant than the
America that Rodó described in the days of Manifest Destiny and gunboat
diplomacy that followed the blatantly jingoist raid that Americans euphemisti-
cally refer to as the Spanish American War. Indeed, the events of the 20th
century have served to reinforce the national myth of superiority. The establishment of unparalleled industrial might, military victories in two world wars
and on both sides of the globe, and the staggering economic defeat of Communism in the Cold War all have combined to cement America's presumption of

---

1. Rodó, *Ariel,* trans. Paden, 121.

1

national superiority and to increase her prideful arrogance. However, these are merely the most recent chapters in a long history of escalating national illusions of pre-eminence and blind national egoism.

Are these presumptions of superiority a product of a runaway nationalism? Or, conversely, does this vigorous nationalism spring from deep-seated convictions of national superiority? The answer is yes to both questions. The relationship between nationalism and traditions of national superiority is circular. That is to say, feelings of national exceptionalism are a universal characteristic of nationalism; and historically embedded national superiority myths and self-serving notions of universal mission fuel the growth of potent varieties of nationalism.

Americans have been, and are today, exposed almost from birth to a particularly virulent strain of nationalism unlike that found in other modern nations. The resulting affliction stems from an unswerving faith in national superiority and uniqueness that is deeply ingrained in the American mind. Historically, these notions of superiority sprang from myths of the unique abundance and regenerative power of the new land; from visions of chosen-ness, mission, and high destiny; from the indelible lessons of frontier self-sufficiency; from a developing sense of American isolation and uniqueness, and finally from the perceived universality of American ideology. In some of us, nationalist feelings are intermittent or limited, but few of us are immune, especially in times of anger, sentimentality[2] or fear; and those of us who strive to cure ourselves do so in full recognition of our affliction's strength and ubiquity.[3] In spite of, and perhaps because of, our many strengths, practically all of us as Americans share this particularly prideful, unlovely, and potentially fatal weakness. In one form or another and to some degree or another, we carry national pride across the invisible boundary that separates benign patriotism from malignant nationalism. Such a crossing constitutes a journey from reason to emotion, from individual liberty to mass tyranny, and from humanity to inhumanity.

This book is an effort to define and diagnose this national disease, to explore its historical, psychological, political, and cultural causes and effects, and to prescribe a cure.

---

2. Orwell, "Notes on Nationalism," in *Collected Essays*, 238.
3. Gellner, *Nationalism*, 9.

INTRODUCTION: MAKING THE WORLD OVER IN AMERICA'S IMAGE

The perspective of José Enrique Rodó, that is to say the view from Latin America, is a very good place to begin our inquiry. In the beginning, Spanish colonials in Latin America shared with their contemporaries in the English colonies to the North an intoxication born of the promise of the New World. They too breathed the air of freedom that blew across virgin lands and promised new beginnings. They too harbored the heady ideals inherent in the possibility of throwing off the yoke of a reactionary and intolerant Old World with its feudal remnants and dead-end societies. Only a few decades after the American Revolution, most of Latin America broke free from Spain, enthusiastically seeking to copy more progressive political and social models in France, England, and especially in the United States.

However, this was not to be on the southern continent; "the vacuum between law and reality was too vast, " and tyrants rushed in to fill it: Santa Anna in Mexico, Rosas in Argentina, Francia in Paraguay.[4] Still, Latin American liberals continued to enthusiastically admire the United States, even though the Monroe Doctrine, which had initially seemed to protect them from Old World colonial intervention, soon became a barrier, depriving liberal revolutionary causes the European help they needed and isolating budding national cultures from the riches of European civilization.[5]

Latin Americans' admiration of the U.S. was soon disappointed. In the 1840s, the United States openly revealed her arrogance by voicing the audacious thesis of Manifest Destiny, based on her long-incubating perceptions of "a provi-

---

4. Fuentes, Prologue to *Ariel* by Rodó, trans. Paden, 15.
5. Fuentes, Prologue to *Ariel* by Rodó, trans. Paden, 15-6.

dential and historically sanctioned right to continental expansion."[6] After her defeat of Mexico in 1848, the U.S. annexed what are now Texas, New Mexico, Arizona, Colorado, Nevada, and California. This action was justified as "the inevitable fulfillment of a moral mission, delegated to the nation by Providence itself."[7] However, when the Constitution did not follow the flag into Old Mexico, it was clear that U.S motives were territorial and did not include an effective liberation of their southern neighbor. Not surprisingly, the view from the southern hemisphere suddenly revealed a "Jekyll and Hyde" America, "a democracy inside, an empire outside."[8]

A half-century later came the Spanish American War, and the United States gobbled up Cuba, Puerto Rico, Guam, Wake Island, and the Philippines. Again, the Constitution did not follow the flag, and again the seizure of these lands was justified by the now expanding doctrine of Manifest Destiny, which by the 1890s included not only the right to continental expansion but also the providential obligation to "lead the world to new and better things."[9] In response to the ensuing Filipino insurrection, Senator Platt of Connecticut voiced the national self-justification in a letter to President McKinley, "God has placed upon this government the solemn duty of providing the people of these islands a government based on the principle of liberty, no matter how many difficulties the problem may present."[10] It was the first exercise in a lesson that the United States has yet to learn. Despite all evidence to the contrary, most Americans, then as now, arrogantly believed that "American sovereignty would be a blessing to any land."[11] For Latin America and for much of the rest of the world, the result of this misguided notion was that the United States "desatanized Spain while satanizing itself."[12]

Rodó is clear in his assessment of all of this, and his appraisal is still valid today:

> As fast as the utilitarian genius of that nation [The United States] takes on a more defined character, franker, narrower yet, with intoxication of material prosperity, so increases the impatience of its sons to spread it abroad by propaganda, and thinks it predestined for all humanity. Today they openly aspire to the primacy of the world's civilization, the direction of its ideas, and think themselves the forerunners of all culture that is to prevail.[13]

---

6. Stephanson, *Manifest Destiny*, xii.
7. Weinberg, *Manifest Destiny*, 1-2.
8. Fuentes, Prologue to *Ariel* by Rodó, trans. Paden, 16.
9. Stephanson, *Manifest Destiny*, xii.
10. Weinberg, *Manifest Destiny*, 290.
11. Stephanson, *Manifest Destiny*, 99.
12. Fuentes, Prologue to *Ariel* by Rodó, trans. Paden, 16.
13. Rodó, *Ariel*, trans. Stinson, 121-3.

American histories of today bear out Rodó's critique. According to US foreign policy historian Michael Hunt, "America entered the 20th century with three images of Latin America at their disposal," that of a "half breed brute" to justify American "aloofness and predatory aggressiveness," a feminine image to cast the US as "ardent suitor and gallant savior," and that of the infantile and often Negroid Latin, to justify America's "tutelage and stern discipline." In each case, Hunt explains, "Americans stood in relation to Latinos as superiors dealing with inferiors." Hunt goes on to assert that, as the 20th century began to unfold, the United States used these images to rationalize and support "the ripening claim of the US to the role of leader and policeman of an American System of states." With Europe fenced out by the Monroe doctrine, Hunt continues, "American policy makers, with inherited pretensions of superiority over Latinos and with ever-increasing power to make good on these pretensions, moved steadily toward making the hemisphere a US preserve."[14] Today critics of contemporary US foreign policy in Central and South America still make the same charges.

But Rodó's critique is not at its heart political, it is cultural. He considers it unthinkable that the US should presume to complete with Europe on a cultural stage.

> At the bottom of this rivalry with Europe lies a contempt ... that is almost naive and the profound conviction that, within a brief period, they [Americans] are destined to eclipse ... [Europe's] glory and do away with its spiritual superiority.... It were useless to seek to convince them that the fire lit upon European alters, the work done by the peoples living these three thousand years ... makes a sum that cannot be equaled by any equation of Washington and Edison.[15]

Like many contemporary foreign critics of American culture, Rodó is scathing in his assessment: "... in the ambient of America's democracy there are no heights so lofty as to escape the flood of vulgarity."[16] Later on, he is quite specific as to the nature of this vulgarity: "the negation of great art, strained brutality of effect, insensibility to soft tones or an exquisite style, the cult of bigness, and that sensationalism which excludes all noble serenity as incompatible with the hurry of his hectic life."[17]

At the start of the 21st century, Rodó's assessment of the "vulgar" culture that the United States strives to export still rings true for many critics. This is particularly poignant because, although the blatant American imperialism of the turn of the last century is now only a memory, today the nation's policies evidence more insidious brands of imperialism: cultural imperialism, economic

---

14. Hunt, *Ideology and US Foreign Policy*, 62.

15. Rodó, *Ariel*, trans. Stinson, 121-3.

16. Rodó, *Ariel*, trans. Stinson, 109.

17. Rodó, *Ariel*, trans. Stinson, 111.

imperialism, moral imperialism, the imperialism of ideology. All are spread by the same national arrogance, the same cock-sure certainly that we are right.

Many nations fear the United States practices a contemporary brand of "soft imperialism," which is engulfing the world under the auspice of economic globalization. Inherent in these fears is the notion that globalization carries with it inevitable Americanization.[18] At the same time, a broader globalization debate rages as to whether American-led globalization will save the Third World or simply exploit it. In spite of such fears, and despite the setbacks, Americans remain convinced that eventually all nations are destined to fall into step and adopt "the American way." All the while, we decry the rigid fundamentalism of our enemies while we remain utterly blind to our own.

Very early on in the American experience, citizens began to harbor the notion that American institutions, values, and way of life were so superior to those of other nations and that their spread throughout the world was inevitable. Despite the now-obvious pluralistic nature of the modern (or post-modern) world, such ideas still engage the American mind. In 2002, US State Department Planning Director Richard Haass, described what he called the doctrine of integration. Its aim is to integrate "other countries and organizations into arrangements that will sustain a world consistent with US interests and values and thereby promote peace, prosperity, and justice." These "arrangements" involve ideas thought to be universal like the rule of law, human rights, private property, and religious tolerance. It is believed that this kind of integration will lead to prosperity, liberalization, and democratization and thus to peace and stability.[19] Surely, this is all well and good and very much in line with America's core values. Still, such a scheme is grounded in the idea of the superiority of our values and the assumption that our culture and institutions will follow on the heels of reform.

For many Americans, the inevitable world victory is as simple as the facts of economics, commerce, and material progress. "Our population, our wealth, ... our manufacturers, and our agricultural resources are all so expanding that the commercial relations of this country will be such that they must come and go with us."[20] Here is the full-brown myth of national economic superiority exuding a shameless pride, the self-satisfied musing of a people who feel that they have materially acquitted themselves so admirably as to "prove their superiority over all peoples."[21]

Others are convinced that the United States possesses "the most perfect form of government ever devised by man;"[22] that US institutions, moral fiber,

18. Prestowitz, *Rouge Nation*, 6.
19. Richard, Haass, "Defining US Foreign Policy in a Post-Post Cold War World," Foreign Policy Association Lecture, April 22, 2002, quoted in Prestowitz, *Rouge Nation*, 41.
20. Senator William M. Stewart quoted in Hayes, *Evolution of Modern Nationalism*, 238.
21. Hayes, *Evolution of Modern Nationalism*, 226.

and ideology are so superior to those of other nations that all will fall prey, not to force but to a superior population, changing their customs until, one by one, the entire world will be drawn to our civilization, our laws, and our culture. As George Boutwell pompously and incorrectly wrote in 1869, "Other nations take by force of arms, ours by force of ideas."[23]

Over the years, the halls of Congress have continued to ring with the same arrogance that inspired Boutwell in the 1860s and inflamed Rodó in 1900. Senator Beveridge waxed poetic in 1898, "Our institutions will follow on the wings of commerce. And American law, American order, American civilization, and the American flag will plant themselves on shores hitherto bloody and benighted, but, by those agencies of God, henceforth to be made beautiful and bright."[24] Or as Tyler Dennett put it in 1922, American policy is "adopted in great ignorance of the actual facts ... and in a blissful and exalted assumption that any race ought to regard conquest by the American people as a superlative blessing."[25]

All of this blindly overlooks the undeniable fact that the transfer of institutions, laws, economic systems and social mores, not to mention entire cultures, from one people to another is not a simple matter. Rodó points to the great fallacy of the evangelical American superiority myth by quoting the 19th-century French historian Jules Michelet: "the transferal of what is natural and spontaneous in one society to another where it has neither natural nor historical roots, ...[is] like attempting to introduce a dead organism into a living one by simple implantation."[26]

None of this is intended to imply that the original core values put forth in the Declaration of Independence and in the Constitution do not represent important steps toward a universal common good. Certainly, Americans have good reason to be proud and to be faithful to the causes of universal liberty and equality. However, such faith must be tempered with a realistic and therefore modest sense of our own significance. We must openly approach the world in a quest for knowledge and certitude,[27] acknowledging that American ideals, values, institutions, and the American way of life are works in progress, not consummate Ultimate Truths.

---

22. Goebel, "A Government of Laws," in Krakau, *American Nation*, 123.

23. George Boutwell, *The New York Herald* (December 30, 1869), quoted in Weinberg, *Manifest Destiny*, 238-9.

24. Albert J. Beveridge, *The Meaning of the Times and Other Speeches* (1908), quoted in Stephanson, *Manifest Destiny*, 99.

25. Tyler Dennett, *Americans in Eastern Asia* (New York, 1922), quoted in Weinberg, *Manifest Destiny*, 299-300.

26. Fuentes, Prologue to *Ariel* by Rodó, trans. Paden, 18.

27. Bloom, *Closing of the American Mind*, 41.

Still, Americans are sure that they, like Woodrow Wilson, have seen "visions that other nations have not seen," and that, accordingly, the United States' mission has always been to become the "light of the world."[28] Indeed, from the very beginning, the American national identity was built on audacious visions of chosen-ness, destiny, and mission. Ronald Reagan was not the first nor the last in a long line of entrenched American visionaries to proclaim American exceptionalism, with its missionary implications of the Puritan "city on the hill," no longer a stationary beacon, but an active force, the "leader of the free world" directing its forces against "empires of evil."[29]

With such visions comes a warning: "the adoption of political and social values ... as a framework for national identification is possible only if these values are based on some source of apparent ultimate truth which confers on them absolute validity — if they can claim universality."[30] If Americans unflinchingly believe that theirs is the single principle of Absolute Truth representing the universal interests of humankind, then any opposition will appear either criminal or inhuman.[31] As Arthur Schlesinger Jr. puts it, "Those who are convinced that they have a monopoly on Truth always feel that they are saving the world when they slaughter heretics. Their object remains the making of the world over in the image of their dogmatic ideology — their goal is a monolithic world, organized on the principle of the infallibility of a single creed."[32] If Americans are so egotistical as to believe that their nation with its gleaming lamp of Ultimate Truth is the envy of the world, then they will perceive no wrong in trying to make the world over in America's image, by whatever means. However, the world is a very complex and diverse place, and Ultimate Truth is a highly elusive and unstable substance. Thus, these are not only very arrogant ideas; they are also very dangerous ideas.

---

28. Stephanson, *Manifest Destiny*, 55.
29. Stephanson, *Manifest Destiny*, 124.
30. Arieli, *Individualism and Nationalism*, 23.
31. Stephanson, *Manifest Destiny*, 119.
32. Arthur M. Schlesinger, Jr., "One Against the Many," in Schlesinger Jr. and White, *Paths of American Thought*, 538.

PART ONE: NOTES ON NATIONALISM

CHAPTER 1: NATIONALISM

America is not alone in her affliction. A worldwide plague of nationalism has been a deadly driving force in the conflict of nations since nations as we know them came to into existence. Today, all modern nations are infected with their own menacing strains of nationalistic fervor; intolerant, self-aggrandizing, militant, overconfident, dogmatic, racial, blind. Nationalism is not unique to the United States. However, nationalism is unique *in* the United States.

Before we examine the singular characteristics specific to American nationalism, it will be useful to briefly explore nationalism in a broad sense. How did this fundamentally irrational pattern of thought come to hold such great sway over so-called "enlightened" nations? Are there different types of nationalism? If so, what are the characteristics of each? Under what conditions does nationalism thrive?

Toward a Definition of Modern Nationalism

In contemporary usage, the term nationalism has become elastic enough to include a wide array of definitions including those based on various characteristics of nationalist belief and those based on surprisingly diverse speculations regarding nationalism's origin and cause. In the broadest view, one must consider that these various definitions are not necessarily exclusive one to the other. They are merely different windows through which we can evaluate different views of this chameleon-like subject. Indeed, the only reasonable conclusion is that nationalism is many things; it flourishes in many conditions; and it springs from many causes.

In her study *Nationalism: Five Roads to Modernity*, Liah Greenfeld traces the development of national identity and nationalism in England, France, Russia,

Germany, and the United States. In each of these nations modern nationalism appeared in a unique form. Nonetheless, Greenfeld's conclusion is powerful, "national identity is simply the identity characteristic of nations, while nationalism is a ... reflection of major components of modernization."[33] But what is nationalism?

In her definition, Liah Greenfeld seeks to distinguish nationalism from other types of identity. At the core of nationalism, according to Greenfeld, is the *idea* of the nation. Nationalism "locates the source of individual identity within a 'people,' which is seen as the bearer of sovereignty, the central object of loyalty, and the basis of collective solidarity." This definition accounts for considerable diversity, for the nature of the "people" can be defined in various ways but is always perceived as "fundamentally homogenous and only superficially divided by lines of status, class, locality, and in some cases ethnicity."[34] This rather erudite and uniquely flexible definition also allows for all the various types of nationalism, which are the subjects of Greenfeld's study.[35]

Perhaps the most accessible definition of modern nationalism is the one given by George Orwell in his essay of the late 1940s, "Notes on Nationalism." Orwell concludes that nationalism is "the habit of identifying oneself with a single nation, ... placing it beyond good and evil, and recognizing no other duty than that of advancing its interests." He points to the fact that such a radical definition forces the creation of a rigid "us and them" mentality, which in turn forces the assumption that "human beings can [must] be classified like insects and that whole blocks of millions or tens of millions of people can [must] be confidently labeled 'good' or 'bad'." Orwell is careful not to confuse nationalism with patriotism, and he correctly notes that both words are used "in so vague a way that any definition is liable to be challenged." Patriotism, he insists, "is devotion to a particular place and a particular way of life, which one believes to be the best in the world but has no wish to force upon other people." Nationalism on the other hand, is aggressive. According to Orwell, it is "inseparable from the desire for power."[36]

Other definitions assert that nationalism feeds on patriotism. Historian Carlton Hayes sees nationalism as a "fusion of patriotism with consciousness of nationality."[37] He describes it as patriotism corrupted, an "exclusively emotional form of patriotism." According to Hayes, with the onset of nationalism, patriotism's "love of country readily turns to hatred of the alien; its desire for prosperity into competition for territory; and its duty to national service is interpreted as a duty to maintain national unity by unquestioning assent to

---

33. Greenfeld, *Nationalism*, 18.
34. Greenfeld, *Nationalism*, 3-4.
35. Greenfeld, *Nationalism*, 11.
36. Orwell, "Notes on Nationalism," in *Collected Essays*, 265-6.
37. Hayes, *Nationalism: A Religion*, quoted in Kecmanovic, Psychology of Ethnonationalism, 15.

every decision of government." Nationalist policy is characterized by the "sacred egoisms" of "selfishness and aggrandizement." Hayes agrees with Orwell as to the nationalist's desire for power: "inside, tighten national bonds by every means of power, ... outside ... make the nation feared and respected." And surely most damning of all, Hayes asserts, "It [nationalism] sacrifices whatever seems necessary of the principles of free speech and free thought" to achieve internal solidarity "and external power and prestige."[38]

Others like Joseph Burke, focus on nationalism's blind side. For Burke, nationalism is "mass identification with narrow, excessive, unreasoning, boastful beliefs in the right and might of one's country over all. Nationalism is to the State what narcissism is to the individual, ... the expression of perverted and pathological self-absorption and pride."[39]

Many scholars have suggested that, in the nationalist mind, the nation has become an "end in itself." B. C. Shafer, for example, defines nationalism as, "the dogma that the individual lives exclusively for the nation with the corollary that the nation is an end in itself, and the doctrine too, that the nation is, or should be, dominant or supreme among other nations and should take aggressive action to that end."[40]

Some definitions are frighteningly harsh. Ernst Gellner calls nationalism, "a cult of discipline, faith, and subordination."[41] While others are restrained. The Royal Institute of International Affairs simply defines nationalism as "a desire to forward the strength, liberty or prosperity of a nation."[42] Lastly, there are attempts at plurality, like that of Dusan Kacmanovic, who asserts that "nationalism is either a concern for one's own nation, a desire to enhance its strength and prestige, or an overestimation, ... exaggerated praise for one's nation."[43]

THE BIRTH OF THE MODERN NATION

In one way or another, all of these definitions are built on our widely-held notions regarding the fundamental nature and origin of modern nations themselves. So, to continue our examination of nationalism, we will do well to examine what exactly we mean by the term "nation."

Certainly on the surface, this seems to be little more than a common sense issue. The idea of a nation is one of those logical, every-day concepts that we all

---

38. Hayes, *Evolution of Modern Nationalism*, 231.
39. Burke, *Tyranny of Malice*, 257-8.
40. Shafer, B. C., *Nationalism: Myth and Reality*, quoted in Kecmanovic, *Psychology of Ethnonationalism*, 16.
41. Gellner, *Nationalism*, 73.
42. Kacmanovic, *Psychology of Ethnonationalism*, 16.
43. Kacmanovic, *Psychology of Ethnonationalism* , 16.

more or less take for granted. Everyone knows what a nation is, so we don't really need a formal definition. Nonetheless, given the fact that seemingly logical modern nations all embrace the murderously illogical ideology of nationalism with its mindless intolerance and blind conformity, it is only natural to ask ourselves if there is not something illogical about the modern idea of a nation. To find the answer, we must take a step back and try to distance ourselves from what we routinely see as obvious.

In *Banal Nationalism*, Michael Billig muses, "There is something decidedly odd about the [modern] nation-state system."[44] Many scholars agree. They insist that our "taken for granted" definitions of nations as geographic, linguistic, ethnic, and cultural groupings do not always hold up when held up to the lights of history and logic. Most historians point to something quite different from what our common sense tells us. Any brief survey of the nations of today's world will quickly reveal numerous exceptions to our common sense assumptions.

For one thing, most of us assume that nations are generally geographically set off one from another by well-defined natural boundaries: oceans, mountain ranges, or great rivers. But this does not universally appear to be the case. For example, some nations are islands, but then some islands contain several nations, like Hispaniola, Borneo or New Guinea. Mountains and other natural boundaries are not always the rule either. Consider most Middle Eastern nations, Poland or the US and Canada for that matter. "Europe," as Billig reminds us, "is dense with boundaries that whirl and loop across mountains, plains, and rivers."[45]

Similarly, the common language concept of national unity fails even the most survey of tests. Take for example India, China, Belgium or Switzerland; all are nations with multiple widely-accepted national languages. In a similar way, a defined ethnic or cultural linkage is also defrocked as the unifying element. One need only consider China, a vast hodgepodge of Asian cultures; or the United States itself, the world's most celebrated and wildly heterogeneous of melting pots. Suddenly the common sense notion of what nations really are and how they evolved appears shaky. "Why Liechtenstein?" Billig asks, and we cannot answer.

Despite all of these seemingly arbitrary and uneven modern national groupings, most people are still inclined to follow our ingrained sense of "history" and insist that national identities, and thus nations, grew largely from ethnic and cultural groupings that had their beginnings in the shadows of history. We might then attempt to explain the recent rise of nationalism and the resulting irregular national groupings as results of an uneven awakening of ancient cultural and ethnic feelings brought on by certain modern, political, economic, and social forces acting upon the older traditional groupings, which still

---

44. Billig, *Banal Nationalism*, 23.
45. Billig, *Banal Nationalism*, 23.

lie at the root national organizational principles. There is some truth in this explanation, but most sociologists today will say that this focus is wrong. As Ernest Gellner puts it, "Nationalism is not an awakening of nations to self-consciousness, it invents nations where they do not exist."[46]

Age-old ethnic and cultural groupings are not the source of modern national groupings. Modern nations are, as Benedict Anderson puts it, "cultural artifacts of a particular kind."[47] Culture, ideology, and ethnicity have recently been cleverly manipulated, and it is this imaginative manipulation at the hands of new political, economic, and social ideologies that accounts for the appearance of modern nations, for modern national identity, and for nationalism.

There is considerable disagreement among scholars as to what these manipulating forces might be, but most agree, "the new form of state provided a series of solutions to problems in a modernizing world."[48] Industrialization, education, a modern military, commercial capitalism, and idealistic republican governments are all cited as propelling the rise of the modern nation-state.[49]

The chronological beginnings of the modern nation-state have been similarly debated. Some say it came as early as the Renaissance, many suggest the 18th century, and some say even later. Liah Greenfeld places modern nationalism's beginning in early sixteenth century England where the word "nation" was first applied, not only to the "elite," but to the whole of the population, the "people." With this shift in definition, "every member of the 'people' partakes of its superior, elite quality, and it is in consequence that a stratified national population is perceived as essentially homogeneous, and the lines of status and class as superficial."[50] Early on English colonists carried this concept to America, but according to Greenfeld, it was not until the 18th century that nationalism spread to Europe from whence it quickly spread to the rest of the world. Greenfeld's study points to English and American nationalism as an individualistic, "civic" sort, while the later appearance of French nationalism, manifested an ambivalent character, displaying characteristics of both "collectivistic" and "civic" nationalism; German and Russian nationalism came even later, and both displayed characteristics of "ethnic" nationalism.[51]

While exactly when and where modern nations and nationalism began remains the subject of debate, by all accounts, it is a relatively recent phenomenon. As Anthony Giddens asserts, the modern nation-state had "no precedent in history"[52] Once again, this cuts across our common sense concept of

---

46. Gellner, *Thought and Change*, 169.
47. Anderson, *Imagined Communities*, 4.
48. Billig, *Banal Nationalism*, 22.
49. Billig, *Banal Nationalism*, 22.
50. Greenfeld, *Nationalism*, 6-7.
51. Greenfeld, *Nationalism*, 14.
52. Giddens, *Social Theory*, 166.

nations. Old maps show France, England, and Spain. Were they not nations in medieval times? The answer is, no, they were not, not in the modern sense of the term. They were not nations because, even though they were loosely ruled by a national monarch who struggled to hold together groups of feudal overlords, the average residents of these areas did not consider themselves Frenchmen, Englishmen, or Spaniards. As Louis XIV reminded us, the king was the state, and not anyone else. The inhabitant of pre-revolutionary France may have thought himself a Britton or a Norman or a Provencal, but it is unlikely that he thought of himself as French. National boundaries were loosely defined, loyalty to the king was a matter of force not conviction, and at the local and regional levels, the political climate was highly changeable. There was no French nation to which people owed allegiance, because there were no French national people.

With the coming of republican forms of government and the idea of the sovereignty of the people, entirely new kinds of ties began to be built between the state, the people, and the territory. At the same time, the industrial revolution was demanding of society more elasticity, more literacy and more unified modes of communication. Here we find the beginning of nationalism and the modern idea of a nation. In *The Social Contract* (1762), Jean Jacques Rousseau presents an unmistakable "nationalist" agenda, although the word had yet to be coined. Rousseau believed that nothing should interfere with the unity of the state. He goes so far as to call for a "civil religion," whose dogmas would be provided by the state. The penalty for disobedience was to be death. For Rousseau the "general will" was supreme; it was "not the individual who possessed inalienable natural rights, but the sovereignty of the people which was inalienable." For Rousseau, the seemingly totalitarian aspect of his "general will" principle could be mitigated if it was "arrived at by counting votes."[53] In all of this Rousseau warned, "We ought not confound negligence with moderation, nor clemency with weakness. To be just," he said, "it is necessary to be severe."[54] And with these words, the fanatical Jacobin nationalism of Robespierre's "reign of virtue" loomed on the threshold of history.

Michael Billig paints a compelling picture of the French political and social landscape as it was shaped by the French Revolution:

> In claiming that sovereignty rests with the nation, the revolutionaries were speaking as if the idea of the "nation" was unproblematic. In reading their words today, it is easy to assume that the term "nation" had a clear concrete signification. At the time of the Revolution, the conventional symbols of nationhood, which are today taken for granted, were not yet in place.... The language in which the Declaration [of the Rights of Man] had been written was only spoken by a minority of the population; ... to the south it was generally incomprehensible. When the Declaration was announced, only a small percentage of those who lived in the territory now recog-

---

53. Bronowski and Mazlish, *Western Intellectual Tradition*, 302.
54. Jean Jacque Rousseau, *Discourse on Political Economy*, 1755, quoted in Bronowski and Mazlish, *Western Intellectual Tradition*, 302.

nized as being France, thought of themselves as being "French".... "the nation" was not a concrete entity, whose existence all citizens could take for granted. It was a project to be attained.[55]

If this is so, then how was the present concept of France as a modern nation produced? There is considerable evidence that France, along with all of the modern nations of the world, began with only the idea of France, an idea that was conceived in a remarkably short time. Its traditions, its history, its national heroes, its language, its culture, everything that went into making a modern nation was either conjured up, or selected for inclusion from much older folk traditions, some of which were drastically modified to fit the needs of the new nation. If the small minority in Paris who were accomplishing and spreading the French Revolution began to think of themselves as French, then it was to be this minority's outlook that was to prevail in creating what was to become France. "Paris was to speak metonymically and literally for the whole of France." [56]

The development of national languages offers a good example of the process. After the French Revolution, the Parisian style of speech was imposed, legally and culturally, as "French." Again Billig explains it well:

> The achievement of national hegemony is well illustrated by the triumph of official languages and suppression of rivals — a triumph which has often accompanied the construction of statehood. [In France] The Rights of Man and the Citizen did not spread the rights of Bretons and Occitans to use their own tongue in the schoolrooms of France: the northern *langue d'oïl* was enforced, with the backing of legal status over the *langue d'oc*.[57]

This prods a fundamental question that again challenges our common sense. Do languages make nations, or do nations make languages? To the extent that sociologists of today are right, and modern nations evolved as described above, then the answer is, at least in large part, the counter-intuitive one — that nations make languages. So it is for all the aspects of national life — traditions, legends, symbols — all were selections from older cultural lore or new creations fashioned to fit a perceived new image and identity of a modern nation.

In *Imagined Communities*, Benedict Anderson argues that before modern nations could be created, they had to be imagined. Modern nations, according to Anderson, are "imagined communities:"

> The nation is to be imagined as a unique entity in terms of time and space. It is imagined as a community stretching through time, with its own past and its own future destiny; it is imagined across space, embracing the inhabitants of a particular territory.[58]

---

55. Billig, *Banal Nationalism*, 25.
56. Billig, *Banal Nationalism*, 27.
57. Billig, *Banal Nationalism*, 27.
58. Billig, *Banal Nationalism*, 70.

Because there are many different ways of imagining a nation, nations are today wildly uneven as we have noted. [59] Following this line of thought, in order to imagine modern nations, it was necessary to image national groupings, as well as national geography, history, traditions, symbols, myths, and national identities as well. It was then necessary to continue to imagine all of this and to spread and reinforce the imagined image of the nation until the imagined nation appeared and finally became real.

With the creation of national symbols and traditions — flags, anthems, myths, etc. — a great emotional bond between the people and the national unit was forged, maintained, and reinforced. The maintenance of this bond is the function of nationalism, the ideology that maintains the modern nation-state. It has been called "the most successful ideology in the world."[60] Nationalist myths and symbols supply "a retrospective pattern of moral values, sociological order, and magical belief, the function of which is to strengthen tradition and endow it with greater value and prestige by tracing it back to a higher, better, more supernatural reality of initial events."[61] Nationalist mythology seeks to place the nation in an "'immemorial past' where its arbitrariness cannot be questioned."[62] As Raymond Williams reminds us, such a jump "is entirely artificial."[63]

The creation of nation-states and their accompanying powerful nationalistic ideologies involves not only "imagining" followed by constant reinforcing or "remembering," it also involves "forgetting." In the daily "banal" process of reinforcement, a homogeneous nation is constantly remembered; cementing the memory of certain of its glorious symbols, history, traditions and antiquity, and forgetting others. Again, take the example of France. The typical Frenchman has forgotten "whether he or rather his ancestors were Gauls, Bretons, Franks, Burgundians, Normans or something else. It is this national Cloud of Unknowing, this blessed amnesia, which makes France."[64]

Also forgotten is the often-violent mechanism of the nation's recent origin. Once a nation is established, it depends, for its continued existence, upon a sort of "collective amnesia." As Billig puts it, the past is forgotten, even "as it is ostensibly being recalled."[65] The nation is constantly "flagged" by emotional, symbolic reminders of national solidarity, uniqueness, and moral superiority, all designed to cement the bond between the people and the political state, the people and

---

59. Anderson, *Imagined Communities*, 6.
60. Birch, *Nationalism and National Integration*, 3.
61. Malinowski, quoted in Brennan, "National Longing for Form," in *Nation and Narration*, ed. Bhabha, 45.
62. Brennan, "National Longing for Form," in *Nation and Narration*, ed. Bhabha, 45.
63. Williams, *The Year 2000*, quoted in Brennan, "National Longing for Form," in Bhabha, *Nation and Narration*, 45
64. Gellner, *Nationalism*, 45.
65. Billig, *Banal Nationalism*, 38.

the homeland, the people and the national ideology. Bonds are also fashioned among all the members of the national group; the imagined homogeneity of the new nation is remembered, while the diversities that do not fit the imagined mold are forgotten. These "flaggings" are "embedded in the routine of life," until finally they become so numerous, so familiar, that they cease to be imagined and are taken for granted, while the ongoing remembering becomes invisible. Thus, the process of remembering is forgotten,[66] and the nation appears natural and timeless. Before long the naturalness and timelessness of national bonds becomes so deeply embedded in contemporary common sense that we fail to recognize the nation demanding our fanatical devotion as an "invented permanency."[67] Quite literally, we have been brainwashed.

Thus manipulated, and indoctrinated with reinforced common sense notions of nationhood, we overlook what Alan Bloom has called "the accidental character of nations"[68] and infer a completely new way of looking at the world: a natural perception of natural nations in a natural world of nations. The constant emotional "flagging" creates in us a deep-rooted loyalty to our own nation, to our fellow nationals, to our homeland, and all that it stands for. We revel in glowing accounts of how our nation came to be; in pastel, mythological renderings of our national history; and in a heartfelt sense of the holiness of our national mission. Worst of all, we begin to harbor vivid illusions of uniqueness, arrogant presumptions of superiority, and irrational animosities toward other national groups along with a blind willingness to sacrifice anything for our national cause. The unrelenting calls for national loyalty and homogeneity seem essential, just as it seems natural to us that national boundaries and national ideologies must be rigorously drawn and fanatically defended.

NATIONAL IDENTITY

Imagining a nation involves the creation of a national identity, a unifying self-image that binds members of the nation by belief in a unique common destiny, unique common strengths, and unique common ideals. This shared national identity links individuals to their fellow nationals to form and cement the national group. At the same time, through the force of nationalism, it projects this national identity back on the nation itself and, in so doing, binds the national group in its devotion to the geographical homeland and to the political state.

Themes of uniqueness are vital in establishing and reinforcing national identity, for its perceived uniqueness allows the national group to define itself by

---

66. Billig, *Banal Nationalism*, 38.
67. Billig, *Banal Nationalism*, 35-6.
68. Bloom, *Closing of the American Mind*, 153.

focusing on its differences from other national groups, which it perceives as inferior. The usual dynamics of group interaction occur here: the need to belong, the need for homogeneity within the group, feelings of safety as a member of the group, and the denigration of other groups. There is considerable stereotyping, especially in negatively defining other national groups as inferior. The specific American national identity, for example, developed in direct opposition to an opposing "other," which has always been characterized as liberty's adversary. First, it was Great Britain, and then all of monarchal Europe. Later it aligned itself with Europe to oppose first fascism, then communism, and finally terrorism. Reaction to such opposition always takes the form of a moral crusade; the United States can only fight on the side of good against evil, "and because the fight is against evil, the victory must be absolute, and surrender unconditional."[69] Unlike most other groups, the identification with the national group requires supreme devotion and demands complete loyalty, overriding all other attachments and loyalties; it must dominate all other feelings of collective identity, including religious identity.[70]

Like the modern concept of the nation, national identity is "flagged" and reinforced by an invisible daily, pageant of national symbols, slogans, myths, and traditions, extolling the national virtues, until the "flagging" becomes transparent and is forgotten. Thus, the national identity appears to be rooted in tradition and in a glorious national history. It takes on an impossibly heroic character; illusions of superiority ensue; and national ends appear to be one with universal truth.

---

69. Prestowitz, *Rogue Nation*, 41.
70. Kecmanovic, *Psychology of Ethnonationalism*, 21-2.

CHAPTER 2: TYPES OF NATIONALISM

Although all nationalism works in more or less the same way, many types of nationalism support today's diverse modern nations. In the broadest overview, most historians separate nationalism into two basic types: ethnic and civic.

As noted, one of the starting points for nationalism is the identification of unique characteristics that can define the national group and distinguish it from other national groups. These characteristics often include language, customs, religion, place of origin, and biological ethnicity. In ethno-nationalistic nations, national identity revolves around primordially fundamental human experiences that appear to be "almost biologically rooted."[71] The ethnic nation is a "folkish" community. It is not necessarily bound by a "common legal code or state boundaries, but by descent, language, customs, and history."[72] Many aspects of these binding "folkish" historical and cultural elements are the products of rather recent national "imaginings."

The other basic form of nationalism is civic nationalism, which is based on "common citizenship, subjugation to the same laws, and habitation in a unified geographic territory."[73] Here, inclusion in the national group is not contingent on ethnicity, language, or other characteristics."[74] Civic nationalism has its roots in England and in the American and the French Revolutions, and it "revolves around a body of citizens whose collective strategy constitutes the state."[75]

All modern nations are a product of, and are sustained by, some combination of these two fundamental types of nationalism. Nonetheless, as Liah

---

71. Cocks, *Passion and Paradox*. 8.
72. Hockenos, *Free to Hate*, 11.
73. Cocks, *Passion and Paradox*, 8.
74. Hockenos, *Free to Hate*, 11.
75. Hockenos, *Free to Hate*, 11.

Greenfeld points out, nationalism can grow in many different political and social ideological environments and incorporate many different ideological underpinnings. At the most fundamental level these ideological differences are based on popular interpretations of sovereignty: either as the "individualistic-libertarian" type as in America and most of the West or as the "collectivistic-authoritarian" type found in totalitarian states. Originally, according to Greenfeld, "nationalism developed *as* democracy, and where conditions of such original development persisted, the identity between the two remained." However, as the idea spread, "the emphasis in the idea of the nation (sometimes) moved from the sovereign character to the uniqueness of the people," and the original equivalence between nationalism and democracy was lost. This new nationalism based on uniqueness reflected a collective being, and "collective ideologies are inherently authoritarian." Thus, both a voluntary "individualistic-libertarian" nationalism can be acquired and an inherent "collectivistic-authoritarian" nationalism that is most often genetic.[76]

A BRIEF HISTORY OF EUROPEAN NATIONALISM

In 1931, Carlton Hayes wrote *The Historical Evolution of Modern Nationalism*. Although modern theory has changed significantly since its publication, this work remains a primary source on the history of European nationalism. Hayes's singular contribution is his historical catalogue of the evolving types of nationalist theory and practice from the beginnings of modern nations in the late 18th century to the early part of the 20th century. These include humanitarian nationalism, Jacobin nationalism, traditional nationalism, liberal nationalism, and integral nationalism. A brief description of each and its place in history will be useful.

Hayes, like most scholars, places the beginnings of nationalism in the 18th century with the beginnings of revolutionary movements for liberty, the rule of law, individual freedom, and the sovereignty of the people. According to Hayes, the spirit of the Enlightenment ran through the first "systematic doctrines" of nationalism. Although nationalist thinkers of the age (Bolingbroke, Rousseau, Herder) differed as to details, all extolled pure reason and natural rights, and all saw nationalism as a strictly humanitarian force, an inevitable step in human progress.[77] This is what Hayes calls humanitarian nationalism. Just as French nationalism had sought to end aristocratic tyranny and privilege, humanitarian nationalism encouraged all peoples to assert their right to self-determination and "strike off the shackles that bound them."[78]

---

76. Greenfeld, *Nationalism*, 10-1.
77. Hayes, *Evolution of Modern Nationalism*, 16-7.
78. Hayes, *Evolution of Modern Nationalism*, 37-8.

But as the French Revolution gained momentum, a new, radical force of nationalism appeared. Hayes calls this Jacobin Nationalism. It was characterized by intolerance of internal dissent, the use of force both internally and eternally, patriotic fanaticism, and the idea that the individual owes supreme loyalty to the state.[79] Here we see the appearance of many modern nationalistic institutions: citizen soldiers, national conscription, the use of public education to instill nationalist dogma, and national emphasis on ritual and homogeneity.

In the wake of the Revolution and the wars that followed, the rest of Europe feared the radical nature of Jacobin Nationalism, and a new reactionary nationalist doctrine appeared. Hayes calls this "traditional nationalism." Traditional nationalism bound the nation, not through revolution and democracy, but by emphasizing traditions, common history, and a pluralist sovereignty, which included the church, the aristocracy, and a hierarchical social order.[80]

As the eighteenth century wore on, the new breed of emerging republican European nations found traditional nationalism too reactionary and Jacobin nationalism far too radical. Thus, according to Hayes, liberal nationalism was born. Liberal nationalism embraced humanitarian, republican ideals and paid lip service to democracy. But in order to field effective armies and strengthen nationalistic bonds, it adopted many of the tools of Jacobin nationalism, like universal military training and the use of public education and popular journalism to further the nationalist cause. Still, it stopped short of the radical single-mindedness and intolerance that had characterized Jacobin nationalism. This liberal, largely romantic doctrine sought to free the oppressed of the world and usher in a new age of liberty, democracy, and self-determination.[81]

Such idealistic notions were difficult to sustain. As Hayes observed, "Once oppressed nationalities had won their independence by force of arms... they came more and more to feel that only force of arms could maintain their independence and insure their rightful place and prestige in the world."[82] With the appearance of such fears came the rise of what Hayes calls "integral nationalism," with its reliance on brute force. Slowly humanitarian nationalism turned selfishly inward, Jacobin and liberal nationalism lost the selfless quality of their missionary zeal, and traditional nationalism disappeared with monarchies and older inflexible class structures. In their place, the nations of Europe, and finally the nations of the world, began to embrace, or at least accept, the rise of so-called integral nationalism, with its "excessive, exaggerated, exclusive emphasis on the value of the nation...."[83]

---

79. Hayes, *Evolution of Modern Nationalism*, 52-83.
80. Hayes, *Evolution of Modern Nationalism*, 110-1.
81. Hayes, *Evolution of Modern Nationalism*, 116
82. Hayes, *Evolution of Modern Nationalism*, 226.
83. Kecmanovic, *Psychology of Ethnonationalism*, 21-2.

Hayes's concept of integral nationalism owes a debt to the French poet and monarchist, Charles Maurras, who in 1900 coined the term as part of his philosophy of "integralism," a kind of "blood and soil" conservatism, which holds that society is an "organic unity." Hayes sums up Maurras's integral nationalism as follows:

> Integral Nationalism is hostile to internationalism preached by the humanitarian and the liberals. It makes the nation not a means to humanity, not a stepping-stone to a new world order, but an end unto itself. It puts national interests above those of the individual and above humanity. It refuses cooperation with other nations except as such cooperation may serve its own interests, whether real or fancied. It is jingoistic, distrusts other nations, labors to exalt one nation at the expense of others, and relies on physical force. It is militant, ... and in domestic affairs, integral nationalism is illiberal and tyrannical.[84]

Maurras's "integral nationalism" included much that was later to appear at the core of fascist ideology. The difference between extreme integral nationalism and fascism is toady hard to sort out since the original ideological meaning of fascism has become impossibly blurred. Owing to the horrors of World War II, almost no one claims to be a fascist anymore, and the term is now most often used simply as pejorative reference to the extreme right.

THE CHARACTERISTICS OF INTEGRAL NATIONALISM

In 1931, Clinton Hayes found integral nationalism in almost all the nations of the world. "The masses in most states today," he wrote, "acquiesce in, and on occasion applaud, public policies which partake of the nature of integral nationalism."[85] In this acquiescence, he found "unpardonable self-deception."[86]

Today, the nations of the world are even more entrenched in integral nationalism than ever, and in many cases what Professor Hayes mistook for "self-deception," now appears to be the result of a kind of national brainwashing, the indoctrination of entire nations into cults of unflinching devotion to the perceived national interest. Even in countries where democratic institutions flourish, the masses often tend toward chauvinism and intolerance with a fanaticism strangely out of keeping with the espoused core beliefs of a free, republican nation.[87] In nations built upon the ideals of liberty and freedom of thought and speech, integral nationalism casts a darkly totalitarian shadow, imposing, in the name of patriotism, the rigid uniformity of nationalistic beliefs on all members of society and, thus, subjugating the individual to an inflexible collective will in

---

84. Hayes, *Evolution of Modern Nationalism*, 165-6.
85. Hayes, *Evolution of Modern Nationalism*, 224.
86. Hayes, *Evolution of Modern Nationalism*, 320-1.
87. Hayes, *Evolution of Modern Nationalism*, 224.

matters of national prestige and security. As Professor Hayes puts it, integral nationalism "would subordinate all personal liberties to its own purpose, and if the common people should murmur, it would abridge democracy and gag it."[88] The state is no longer viewed as a means to achieve moral good, but a moral good in itself, "higher than justice, truth, and honor, all of which it at times sacrifices.[89]

Today integral nationalism is characterized by unbending rigidly, simplistic, black and white moralist certainty and strict uniformity of belief and purpose, all focused directly on the value of the nation and righteousness of the national cause. National myths of superiority and notions of divine sanction are its foundations. The world of integral nationalism is an emotional, populist, intolerant world of sacrosanct traditions and closely guarded boundaries. Above all, it is a world of unquestioned loyalty to the state.

Writing in 1931, Clinton Hayes found "integral nationalism far advanced among us."[90] Although he had probably never heard of José Enrique Rodó, there is no doubt that, in very different language and from a very different point of view, Professor Hayes was echoing some of the same charges against the United States that Rodó had voiced thirty years before. Thirty years after Clinton Hayes wrote, the voice of Joseph McCarthy would still be fresh in the national ear. The Cold War would incubate in a new strain of American nationalism more virulent than any that had gone before. Although the voice of dissent briefly reverberated during the Viet Nam era, the great Middle American majority has never viewed protest as anything other than anti-American. "Our boys are dying over there," the outraged national voice told the protesters, as if this were a compelling reason to support the war. Never mind that the dissenters might have been right. Right or wrong, they were disloyal; they had questioned the ethic of the national cause; they had dared to oppose a core national value. "America, love it, or leave it," everyone had said, and it was clear what this phrase really meant. It was a command for silence, for blind obedience and unflinching dedication to the national cause, no matter what it might happen to be. It is still widely invoked today, a most un-American edict, vehemently issued and sanctimoniously justified by the arrogant presumption of indubitable American infallibility and superiority.

How did the United States come to dare such fundamentalist audacity? In many ways, the entire history of the United States has served to convince the people that their nation is morally, politically, economically, and socially superior to all of the nations of the earth. And since the United States is a nation of the people, it logically follows that Americans, as a people, are individually, severally, and collectively superior to all the peoples of the earth. In many

---

88. Hayes, *Evolution of Modern Nationalism*, 166.
89. Weinberg, *Manifest Destiny*, 411.
90. Hayes, *Evolution of Modern Nationalism*.

respects, Americans have come by their feelings of superiority honestly. Indeed, given the national historical experience, it is hard to be an American and not entertain such notions.

PART TWO: THE EVOLUTION OF THE AMERICAN SUPERIORITY MYTH

CHAPTER 3: THE NEW WORLD

Many aspects of the American experience have combined to create our deeply embedded notions of national superiority. The first, and one of the most influential of these, involves our historical perceptions of the new land itself. The sudden appearance of a lush, bountiful, and seemingly boundless new world fascinated the European mind and precipitated unprecedented speculations. As the Dutch historian Henri Baudet has written, America soon became a place "onto which all identification and interpretation, all dissatisfaction and desire, all nostalgia and idealism seeking expression could be projected."[91]

THE MYTH OF THE GARDEN

Stumbling up out of the mists of prehistory, Europeans carried with them primal myths of a hero's journey to a magical land apart from the world, an enchanted wilderness or an ethereal garden. Here the hero penetrated some mystical, life-enhancing source of power.[92] These myths gave rise to a whole series of idealized imaginary worlds: Arcadia, Elysium, Atlantis, and the enchanted gardens of Eden and Tirnanogue.[93] No doubt such myths were, at least in part, the product of a fearful European world bending under "disease, poverty, and disorder," weights that drove the European imagination to visions a distant paradise.[94] Columbus, himself had speculated on his third voyage that he was nearing the "spot of earthy paradise."[95] In all of this, there persisted the idea of

91. Buadet, *Paradise of Earth*, 55.
92. Marx, *Machine in the Garden*, 228.
93. Marx, *Machine in the Garden*, 39-40.
94. Greene, *Intellectual Construction of America*, 25.

withdrawing from the real world to begin a new life in a fresh green landscape.[96] As Leo Marx puts it, "Centuries of longing and reverie had been invested in the conception."[97]

And then, quite unexpectedly, at the end of the 15th century, Europe was confronted with the reality of a vast new world, a virgin wilderness far across the sea, "the last and greatest of all human dreams." Standing "face to face for the last time in history with something commensurate with ... [its] capacity for wonder,"[98] the European mind was dazzled. Suddenly the appearance of two great, unspoiled continents gave rise to the possibility that "mankind might actually realize what had been thought a poetic fantasy. Soon the dream of a retreat to an oasis of harmony and joy was removed from its traditional literary context."[99]

And so there evolved a vision of America as a new beginning, a vision that embraced the idea that men could be regenerated in the New World, that they could become better and happier, that they could be reborn.[100] Like the primal myth of the hero's journey, the new American myth held that the source of this rebirth and of "special virtue" was to be found in the land itself, in "access to undefiled, bountiful, sublime Nature.... The landscape thus ... [became] the ideal repository for all kinds of goodness — economic, political, aesthetic, religious."[101] Notions of national goodness and superiority flowing from the land itself have always held a firm grip on the American mind.

The idea that America might become Arcadia fascinated Europeans, and throughout the 17th century, descriptions taken from Virgil were routinely employed to describe the new continent.[102] Some scholars speculate that the magical island in Shakespeare's *The Tempest* depicts a New World setting. Whatever the case, there can be little doubt that the play mirrors the accumulating American imagination. As Leo Marx puts it, "the imaginative authority of the fable arises from the seriousness and wonder with which Shakespeare is able to depict a highly civilized man testing his powers in a green and desolate wilderness."[103]

Across the Atlantic in the New World itself, the early settler often felt a kind of resurrection despite his hardships. In Europe, "he had not lived, but

---

95. Christopher Columbus, *Selected Letters of Columbus*, 137, quoted Greene, *Intellectual Construction of America*, 26.

96. Marx, *Machine in the Garden*, 3.

97. Marx, *Machine in the Garden*, 39-40.

98. Fitzgerald, F. Scott, *The Great Gatsby*, quoted in Marx, *Machine in the Garden*, 360.

99. Marx, *Machine in the Garden*, 3.

100. Marx, *Machine in the Garden*, 228.

101. Marx, *Machine in the Garden*, 228.

102. Marx, *Machine in the Garden*, 39.

103. Marx, *Machine in the Garden*, 68.

simply vegetated; he now feels himself a man; ... he begins to forget his servitude, and dependence; his heart involuntarily swells and grows."[104] The American landscape meant regeneration to the European peasant. It offered a simple man a chance he could not have known in Europe. For the farmer, the land was the source of his "secular, egalitarian, naturalistic 'resurrection.'"[105]

As more settlers arrived and put the virgin soil to the plow, the symbolically embellished myth of rebirth evolved to encompass the myth of the garden. This idea is still deeply embedded in the American psyche. "The image of this vast and constantly growing agricultural society ... became ... a collective representation, a poetic idea ... that defined the promise of American life. The master symbol of the garden embraces a cluster of metaphors expressing fecundity, growth, increase, and blissful labor on earth."[106] We might also here add "superiority," for looking back on the turmoil and toils of Europe gave rise to inevitable feelings of superiority in the "new race" of farmers who were being reborn in this seemingly mythical land of the promise.

In the glow of these blossoming myths of hope and renewal, it was only natural that Americans should assign to Europe a role of "despair and decay." Cotton Mather writes of "flying from the depravation of Europe to the American strand."[107] Here we find the roots of American xenophobia, the ubiquitous handmaiden of national superiority. These very same roots would also nurture American longings for independence and her future embrace of isolationism. "Almost from the beginning, the New World has repudiated the Old, defining its own virtues as the precise antithesis of the supposed vices of Europe."[108] As the settlers pressed further inland, expanding the frontier, they moved steadily closer to the land and away from what they viewed as the corrupting influence of Europe.[109] So began the long process that Liah Greenfield calls, "the un-universalization of European values." In the end, the rights of the colonists would no longer be "guaranteed by the British constitution, but by the Laws of Nature," which Americans would claim "not by virtue of being English but by virtue of being human."[110]

Thomas Paine came to America from England in 1774, and he was immediately struck by the regenerative power of the New World. "The case and circum-

---

104. Lasky, "America and Europe," in Schlesinger Jr. and White, *Paths of American Thought*, 468-9.

105. Marx, *Machine in the Garden*, 111.

106. Henry Nash Smith, *The Virgin Land*, 123, quoted in Marx, *Machine in the Garden*, 142.

107. Lasky, "America and Europe," in Schlesinger Jr. and White, *Paths of American Thought*, 468-9.

108. Cunliffe, "European Images of America," in Schlesinger Jr. and White, *Paths of American Thought*, 510.

109. Turner, *Frontier in American History*, 4.

110. Greenfield, "American Nationalism," in Krakau, *American Nation*, 31.

stance in America," he wrote in a 1776 pamphlet, "present themselves as in the beginning of the world." Paine's very first impressions of America included a distinct sense of freedom from the corruptions of Europe. "... even the air of the Atlantic disagrees with the constitution of foreign vices," he wrote, in 1775, "if they survive the voyage, they either expire on their arrival, or linger away in an incurable consumption."[111] It did not take Paine long to do what American settlers had intellectually been doing since the Mayflower: connecting American freedom to the land itself. In the *Intellectual Construction of America*, Jack Greene writes:

> Like so many other contributors to the intellectual construction of America, Paine found that happy something in the extensive space and opportunity that America offered. No "country in the world" it seemed to him, provided, "so many openings to happiness." "The vastness of its extent, the variety of the climate, the fertility of the soil, the yet unexplored treasures of its bowels, the multitude of its rivers, lakes, bays, inlets, and other conveniences of navigation" all combined, Paine thought, to make America "one of the richest [and most inviting] subjects of cultivation ever presented to any people upon earth" and to produce societies that varied fundamentally form those of the Old World. Whereas Europe had a numerous "class of poor and wretched people," America did not. Whereas Europe was a world "wrapt up in the most absurd species of slavery," in America all free people enjoyed "all the natural and civil rights" and quickly learned that there was "no such thing ... as power of any kind, independent of the people" and "no other race of men ... but the people."[112]

In the mind of Thomas Paine, America reshaped the human spirit, and his writings are filled with illusions to this transformation. "While men remained in Europe as subjects of some hereditary potentate they had ideas conformable to that condition, but when they arrived in America they" encountered "great ideas."[113] This notion was the springboard for Paine's famous pamphlet, *Common Sense*, which represented perhaps the best statement of the rising colonial American faith in the regenerative power of the new land—"the power to begin the world anew," as Paine so forcefully put it. From this revolutionary concept it was not a great leap for Paine to conclude *Common Sense* by declaring the "cause of America" to be "the cause of mankind."[114]

The American myth of new beginnings in an idyllic, enchanted garden excited fanciful Utopian schemes. Many, like Paine, went so far as to suggest that the new land would become the site of a new beginning for all of Western society.[115] Utopian visions were popular in Europe, and they naturally had a

---

111. Thomas Paine, *Complete Writings*, 1:376, 2:1110, quoted in Greene, *Intellectual Construction of America*, 132.
112. Greene, *Intellectual Construction of America*, 134; Paine, *Complete Writings*, 2:39, 337, 244, 451-2, quoted in Greene, *Intellectual Construction of America*, 134.
113. Paine, *Complete Writings*, 1:354, quoted in Greene, *Intellectual Construction of America*, 134.
114. Paine, "*Common Sense*, in *Complete Writings*, 1:21, 30-1, 123, quoted in Greene, *Intellectual Construction of America*, 135.

strong effect in America. Thomas More's *Utopia* was based at least in part, on the travels of Americus Vespucci. In *The Intellectual Construction of America*, Jack Greene writes, "Through Jonathan Swift and beyond, utopian writers continued to identify the dream of a perfect society with America and to locate their fairy-lands, their New Atlantis, their City of the Sun in some place distant from Europe and in the vicinity of America."[116] Green's scholarship concerning the nature of European utopian visions of the era explores the intellectual soil in which the American superiority myth first began to sprout:

> That tradition consisted of several types of utopias, ranging from pastoral arcadias to perfect commonwealths to millennial kingdoms of God. Whatever their form, however, they all betrayed "deep dissatisfaction" with contemporary Europe and were intended, in More's words, as "example[s] for correction" of European errors. Having expressed this dissatisfaction, before the discovery of America, in their "longing to return to ... the lost Christian paradise, or to the Golden Age of the ancients," Europeans now exchanged this desire for "a world remote in time" for one distant in space. Arcadia, Eden, the New Jerusalem, the scientifically advanced and dominant Bensalem created by Francis Bacon now could be plausibly located in America. In their good order, just government, supportive society, peaceful abundance, and absence of greed, vice, private property, and lawsuits, these happy social constructions, situated by their authors in the New World, served as the antithesis of the Old.[117]

America would be the site of numerous Utopian experiments, in fact, many considered the creation of The United States itself a Utopian experiment. But for most, escape to the New World involved only the simple Utopian theme of pastoral harmony embodied in the land itself and its promise of material abundance. These notions have always been dear to the American heart. Thomas Paine knew his audience when, in *Common Sense*, he described the "brotherhood" of the first settlers:

> The wants which necessarily accompany the cultivation of a wilderness produced among them a state of society.... In such a situation man becomes what he ought. He sees his species ... as kindred; and the example shows to the artificial world, that man must go back to nature for example.[118]

Here we find yet another root of American notions of superior goodness. Since the Renaissance, humankind had been considered inherently good. According to Enlightenment thinkers, like Jean Jacque Rousseau, this goodness was best evidenced in "natural man" or in "man in the state of nature." Evil, Rousseau said, was a perversion that came with civilization. The emerging

---

115. Marx, *Machine in the Garden*, 3.

116. Greene, *Intellectual Construction of America*, 28.

117. Eliot, *Old World and the New*, 26; More, *Complete Works*, 55; Eliot, *Old World and the New*, 25; Jones, *O Strange New World*, 14-21, 35-6; Davis, *Utopia and the Ideal Society*, 20-23; Bacon, "New Atlantis;" quoted in Greene, *Intellectual Construction of America*, 29.

118. Thomas Paine, *Common Sense*, 1776.

American mind clung to Rousseau's notion of the goodness of natural man and to Enlightenment ideas concerning human perfectibility with their lofty preoccupations concerning "the betterment of mankind." Thomas Paine's words fell on receptive ears when he called for revolutionary steps that would render America "the glory of the earth."[119] These words embodied philosophies of hope, and they captured the imagination of a continent, inspiring a new breed of "natural men" who saw themselves as a collective "new Adam, free from the tainted nature of all who lived before."[120] American Revolutionaries regarded their cause as Promethean and looked to themselves for the strength to turn a wilderness into a garden and to "begin the world over again,"[121] as Paine had instructed. This new breed sired Jefferson's cherished superior breed of democratic Americans, the yeoman farmer.

THE NEW CANAAN

Visions of the New World as a place of rebirth in a magical garden where not the only myths to be attached to the new land. The first settlers were religious men seeking sanctuary, and they saw in America a New Canaan. Europeans of the 16th century considered any land not occupied by Christians to be free for the taking. Certainly, the expanding of Christendom was considered a sacred mission, but only the New England Puritans considered the land itself to be sacred. The early Puritans colonists saw themselves as the re-enactors of the Exodus narrative. They embraced "a powerful theology of chosen-ness that was to be decisive for the course of colonization, as well as for the later American self-concept." In the Puritan mind, the Jews had been denied the favor of God when they refused the Gospel; a regeneration had taken place in the Reformation; and English Puritans had taken up the mantel when they sought to establish their "New Israel" in America. [122]

Although the Puritans saw America as a new "Promised Land" and themselves as a new "Chosen People" re-living the Old Testament epic, most of the other ideas they brought to the New World were New Testament to the core. When Luther proclaimed his "priesthood of all believers," he had insisted, "neither Pope, nor bishop, nor any other man has the right to impose a single syllable of law upon a Christian man without his consent."[123] As Vernon Parrington puts it, "There was gunpowder packed away in Luther's priesthood of all believers."[124] Although Luther intended it as a solely ecclesiastical explosive,

---

119. Thomas Paine, *Common Sense*, 1776.
120. Furay, *Grass-roots Mind in America*, 9; Lewis, *American Adam*.
121. Thomas Paine, *Common Sense*, 1776.
122. Stephanson, *Manifest Destiny*, 6.
123. Parrington, *Main Currents*, 1:12.

this volatile rhetoric would eventually blow down the walls of repression and tyranny across the entire sweep of human endeavor. In the New World, Luther's compelling, liberal, religious concepts underwent a dynamic fusion with secular concepts and republican ideologies. "Visions of the United States as a sacred space providentially selected for divine purposes found counterpart in the secular idea of the new nation of liberty as a privileged stage for the exhibition of a new world order, a great experiment to benefit mankind as a whole."[125] The land and the people fused into one idea, one myth: a glorious myth of hope. How could they not feel superior?

THE FRONTIER

Beyond the ethereal powers of myth, religion, and lofty ideals, there was real power in the new American landscape. As the colonist pressed deeper into the virgin wilderness, the land itself began to shape men in revolutionary ways. Woodrow Wilson understood the force of the expanding American frontier: "The great pressure of people moving always to new frontiers, in search of new lands, the full freedom of a virgin world has ruled our course and formed our policies like a Fate."[126]

Embedded deep in the European psyche, there had always been the notion that a single dominant people would carry civilization forward and that the course of their progress would be always westward.[127] Americans remain taunted by this notion when they idealize the American west. Yehoshua Arieli puts it well:

> The vast empty spaces, unobstructed by the past, invited men to live freely and not in crowds. Here the eternal beneficence of nature could be observed, and reason became the guide of action. Unhampered by the accumulations of custom, prejudice, and the follies and crimes of the ages, men could work out their own salvation by their own powers. Here humanity was re-created anew as one race out of a mixture of nations and religions. Here the process of civilization was repeated in the space of a few generations.[128]

The "re-creation of civilization" on the American frontier would yield something new and untested. Parrington reminds us that the frontiersmen were clearing away a great deal more than "the great oaks and maples of the virgin wilderness;" they were "uprooting ancient habits of thought, destroying social customs that had grown old and dignified in class-ridden Europe."[129] In his

---

124. Parrington, *Main Currents*, 1:6.
125. Stephanson, *Manifest Destiny*, 5.
126. Woodrow Wilson, "Ideals of America," *Atlantic Monthly*, XC, 1902.
127. Stephanson, *Manifest Destiny*, 18.
128. Arieli, *Individualism and Nationalism*, 42.

fantasy, "Earth's Holocaust," Nathaniel Hawthorne, manages to capture this leveling incendiary spirit, by tapping the prevailing American "impulse to escape
from every existing mode of organizing and explaining experience, in order to
confront life on entirely original terms." Thoreau addressed this same American
need while reflecting on "the essential facts of life" at Walden Pond. Both Hawthorne and Thoreau understood America's impulse to "purgatorial action — pre-
ceding, as it were, the life of the new Adam in a new earthly paradise."[130]

"On the frontier," as Fredrick Jackson Turner puts it, "the bonds of custom
are broken and unrestraint is triumphant." Turner saw the frontier as "a great
escape from the bondage of the past," producing "scorn for the older society,
...impatience in its restraints and ideas, and indifference to its lessons."[131] "Individualistic and democratic tendencies were emphasized ... by wilderness conditions," Turner wrote.[132] He proposed that the new land and the condition of the
frontier implanted in each American soul a new spirit: the self-reliant, self-proclaimed, self-superior spirit of American democratic individualism.

It was not a great leap from the notion of the frontier as the crucible of
American individualism and democracy to the notion of the frontier as the forge
of American superiority. Turner and many others have romanticized the figure of
the American frontiersman, that aggressive, restless, pioneer with his axe and
Winchester. From the very beginning of the Westward migration, Turner
describes the "common traits" found in the American frontiersman "to which the
American intellect owes its striking characteristics:"

> That coarseness and strength combined with acuteness and inquisitiveness; that
> practical, inventive turn of mind, quick to find expedients; that masterful grasp of
> material things, lacking in the artistic but powerful to effect great ends; that rest-
> less, nervous energy; that dominant individualism, working for good or for evil, and
> withal that buoyancy and exuberance which comes form freedom — these are the
> traits of the frontier or traits that called out elsewhere because of the existence of
> the frontier.[133]

Such traits combined to create superior individuals in a distinctively Darwinian mold, men of "activity" and "inventiveness," men who "honored the man
whose eye was the quickest and whose grasp was the strongest."[134] The frontier,
according to Turner, was the training ground for that superior breed of
American, the captain of industry:

> Into this region flowed the great forces of modern capitalism. Indeed, the region
> itself furnished favorable conditions for the creation of these forces, trained many of

---

129. Parrington, *Main Currents*, 1:133.
130. Lewis, *American Adam*, 14.
131. Turner, *Frontier in American History*, 38.
132. Turner, *Frontier in American History*, 65.
133. Turner, *Frontier in American History*, 37.
134. Turner, *Frontier in American History*, 153.

the famous American industrial leaders. The Prairies of the Great Plains, and the Great Lakes furnished new standards of industrial measurement. From the society, seated amidst a wealth of material advantages, and breeding individualism, energetic competition, inventiveness, and spaciousness of design, came the triumph of the strongest. The captains of industry arose and seized nature's gifts. Struggling with one another, increasing the scope of their ambitions as the largeness of the resources and the extent of the fields of activity revealed themselves, they were forced to accept the material conditions as a province vast in area but simple in structure.[135]

For Fredrick Jackson Turner, the American frontier wrought the American national character from the ideal of the pioneer. In Turner's mind, the frontier experience had represented an "evolution and adaptation" in response to a changing environment. In many ways, his is a history of the origin of new superior political species.

In *American Exceptionalism* Arnon Gutfeld presents an examination of Turner and his critics. He writes that in the myths of the frontier many Americans find unique notions of a national destiny propelled by the ability of a people to "extricate themselves from a previously subordinate state and take control of the physical and human world around them." According to Gutfeld, many viewed the American West as "a testing ground for examining the way in which one group of people was superior to another and to nature."[136]

As the frontier moved westward, the plentiful natural resources of the new continent were a source of wonder to all. They were taken as a sign of God's favor, and "linked to the goodness of the people and to American uniqueness" which included not only superior virtue, but also a sense of "superior well-being."[137] With his growing self-reliance, the American frontiersman began to see the virgin land as a something to be shaped according to his own design.[138] The wilderness became precious for "what could be made of it."[139] And when the original frontier was gone, new frontiers appeared—frontiers of industry, technology, and change. These too would contain resources ripe for exploitation and every bit as rich as those harvested from bounty of the virgin land. From the riches of the land, the growth of American individualism, and the increasing national mastery of technology came a vision of American progress, which contained the egotistical notion that Americans could "understand and control history."[140]

---

135. Turner, *Frontier in American History*, 154.
136. Gutfeld, *American Exceptionalism*, 19.
137. Greenfeld, "American Nationalism," in Krakau, *American Nation*, 24.
138. Lasch, *Culture of Narcissism*, 10.
139. Marx, *Machine in the Garden*, 142.
140. Marx, *Machine in the Garden*, 181.

Such notions would remain a part of the American ethos long after the original frontier disappeared. Gutfeld emphasizes the importance of the seemly inexhaustible bounty of the frontier in the shaping of American myth and ethos.

> Americans venerated the myths of free enterprise and equality of opportunity together with the individual material advancement offered by abundance and the frontier experience—the frontier which for most of American history before the beginning of the twentieth century has served as an effective psychological safety value, symbolizing opportunities of economic betterment and upward social mobility. The abundance of land and the positive relation between human and natural resources highlighted differences in comparison with Europe, where the population was comparatively large and resources were relatively meager. In the consciousness of many, the vast resources and the "free" land became closely tied to individual success and were the foundation of for numerous American myths.[141]

These myths survive today in mutated American visions of progress, opportunity, equality, and superiority. For Gutfeld, the closing of the American frontier constituted "the greatest trauma in the history of American exceptionalism." He insists that it "exposed the effective components of the American ethos," revealing forces that were shaping the evolving American culture. Among these components were "plenty, American victory over nature, and American supremacy over other societies."[142]

---

141. Gutfeld, *American Exceptionalism*, xvi-xvii.
142. Gutfeld, *American Exceptionalism*, 27.

CHAPTER 4: CHOSEN-NESS, MISSION, AND DESTINY

American visions of rebirth in a "New Canaan" followed by the remarkable human alchemy accomplished in the crucible of the American frontier combined to produce a self-proclaimed new breed of men who reveled in self-reliance, self-esteem, and superiority. The new land seemed an enchanted place, a land chosen by God with magical powers to shape the human spirit. This perceived regenerative power of the land, together with the Puritan legacy of chosen-ness, laid the foundation for what was to become America's enduring faith in a providential destiny.

THE FINGER OF GOD

The Puritans sought an uncorrupted land not only spatially separate from the Old World, but spiritually separate from Old World ways: "a bastion for the true religion, ... a source of its expansion, a place divinely singled out for higher missions."[143] In their eyes, the Old World had not broken with its satanic ways. They saw themselves as emissaries of divine purpose, later-day biblical travelers living out a miracle of preordained, predetermined, providential destiny following the resurgence of the true faith in the Reformation. Their "predestined, redemptive role" was that of "God's chosen people in the Promised Land."[144] As Deborah Masden points out in *American Exceptionalism*, Puritan notions of chosen-ness were not centered solely on God's selection of individuals into the so-called "visible sainthood." There was also a collective aspect of Puritan chosen-ness,

---

143. Stephanson, *Manifest Destiny*, 3-4.
144. Stephanson, *Manifest Destiny*, 5.

manifest in the "redeemer nation," a community of the chosen. The Puritans in the Massachusetts Bay Colony thought themselves to be nothing less than a community of the saved "singled out by God ... and charged with a special destiny—to establish the conditions of a pure and uncorrupted church that would ensure the salvation of all Christians."[145] "There was throughout this first century of American intellectual consciousness a prophetical identification of America with the judgment of righteousness."[146] This elitist notion formed the inner core of America's enduring superiority complex.

Nonetheless, there is nothing particularly remarkable about the Puritan's journey when one considers their then radical beliefs and their persecution under the Stewart Kings in England in the first half of the 17th century. What is notable, however, is how quickly their solely religious ideals of freedom and destiny gained secular counterpart in the New World. In 1616, a prospectus published in England promised prospective immigrants that they would "go up at once as a ... people marked and chosen by the finger of God."[147] By the middle of the 17th century, the purely religious notion of the "Chosen People" and the "Promised Land" had found broad secular expression.[148] Like the Puritan's sacred journey, America's secular journey was seen as providential, a predetermined history "whose end was to be played out in the specially designed space of America."[149] As the experience of liberty, equality, and dignity began to characterize the new society, it all quickly came to be viewed, not just as the fulfillment of history, but as "the highest stage of history, God's plan incarnate."[150] Visions of the New World suddenly included both a holy "City of God" and a secular "Utopia."

So, from the ecclesiastical root of faith in divine selection, the secular bramble of perceived superiority quickly blossomed. It spread across the new land nourished by visions of "high destiny,"[151] and "a broadly conceived belief in chosen-ness, ... special responsibility and mission."[152] The perceived mission, which began as one of religious evangelism, soon grew to include political, moral, and social values as well. Meanwhile, the Puritan matrix was projected onto more recent bourgeois models of enlightenment and profit.[153]

---

145. Madsen, *American Exceptionalism*, 3.
146. Lasky, "America and Europe," in Schlesinger Jr. and White, *Paths of American Thought*, 468-9.
147. Prospectus (1616) quoted in Stephanson, *Manifest Destiny*, xii.
148. Greenfeld, "American Nationalism," in Krakau, *American Nation*, 24.
149. Stephanson, *Manifest Destiny*, 39-40.
150. Stephanson, *Manifest Destiny*, 39-40.
151. Rossiter, *The American Quest*, 44.
152. Krakau, Introduction to *American Nation*, edited by Krakau, 11.
153. Stephanson, *Manifest Destiny*, 21.

In this regard, Max Weber's insights into the birth of Protestantism are apt. In *The Protestant Ethic and the Spirit of Capitalism*, Weber theorized that the Reformation brought a "calculative form of salvation through disciplined work," which sanctified character traits required by modern capitalism—traits like thrift, entrepreneurial drive, and the ability to accumulate wealth.[154] This goes a long way toward explaining the hasty American refashioning of religious providential destiny into a purely secular force. In the American mind, material progress and the natural abundance of the land gave testament to the new nation's divine sanction. After the Revolution, providential and republican ideals quickly fused, resulting in "a most dynamic combination of sacred and secular concepts," and giving rise to a widespread notion that America was to be the "privileged stage for the exhibition of a new world order, a great experiment to benefit mankind as a whole."[155] This gave new meaning to the old Puritan concept of the "redeemer nation."

THE LIGHT OF THE WORLD

For an ideal to become a sacred mission, to unify and bind a nation, to inspire unflinching service above all other ideals, it must be perceived as a universal truth. American examples of the perceived universality of her national meaning and mission are plentiful and manifest. John Winthrop envisioned "a beacon for all Christendom." This religious image, along with his gleaming "city on the hill" almost immediately became enduring secular metaphors. Loren Bartiz points to the lasting effect of Winthrop's words:

> The myth of the city on the hill became the foundation for the ritualistic thinking of later generations of Americans. This myth helped to establish nationalistic orthodoxy in America. It began to set an American dogma, to fix the limits of thought for Americans about themselves and about the rest of the world, and offered a choice about the appropriate relationships between us and them.[156]

Later Jonathan Edwards would speak of American Puritanism as "the glorious renovator of the world," and the nation would be quick to seize on the phrase with broad reference to liberty, democracy, and equality. And still later, John Adams wrote, "I have always considered the settlement of America ... as the opening of a grand scheme ... for the illumination and emancipation of mankind all over the world."[157] Thomas Paine called the American Revolution, "a beam of light over the world, which reaches unto man."[158] Even Alexander Hamilton

---

154. Cahoone, *Modernism to Postmodernism*, 127.
155. Stephanson, *Manifest Destiny*, 5.
156. Bartiz, "God's Country and American Know-How," 474.
157. John Adams, Notes for "A Dissertation on the Canon and Feudal Law" (1765).

reluctantly acknowledged the notion of America as a universal ideal, when he wrote, "It seems to have been reserved to the people of this country ... to decide the important question whether societies of men are really capable or not of establishing good government from reflection and choice."[159] Jefferson spoke of an "empire of liberty," and the liberation of universal man.[160]

At the time of the Revolution, notions of the universality of the American cause were not limited to New World thinkers. Many observers in Europe caught wind of the powerful appeal of America's quest for liberty. English social radicals were quick to seize on the broad appeal of the new nation's lofty ideals. The British philosopher Richard Price speculated that the American Revolution might "begin a new era in the annals of mankind."[161] "Next to the introduction of Christianity among mankind," Price opined, "[the American] revolution may prove to be the most important step in the progressive course of human development."[162] The French economist, M. Turgot, called America "the hope of the world," in 1778,[163] and three years later his philosopher-countryman, Abbé Raynal, observed that America had made her cause "that of the whole human race."[164]

As, America grew, the absolute universality of the American cause remained fixed in the national mind. Emerson called the United States the "last effort of Divine Providence on behalf of the human race."[165] Hawthorne, Melville, and Whitman "all savored a powerful argument for America having brought a new dawn."[166] "We Americans are the Peculiar Chosen People—the Israel of our time. We bear the ark of the liberties of the world," Melville would write in 1849.[167] Woodrow Wilson waxed poetic on the universal mission of America when he declared the nation to be "the light of the world, ...destined to set a responsible example to all the world of what free government is and can do."[168]

---

158. Paine, *Complete Writings*, 1:239-40, quoted in Greene, *Intellectual Construction of America*, 138.
159. Alexander Hamilton quoted in Introduction to *American Nation*, edited by Krakau, 12.
160. Stephanson, *Manifest Destiny*, 22.
161. Price, *Observations on the Importance of the American Revolution*, 173, quoted in Greene, *Intellectual Construction of America*, 139.
162. Price, *Observations on the Importance of the American Revolution*, 173, quoted in Greene, *Intellectual Construction of America*, 138.
163. M. Turgot, letter to Richard Price, in Price, *Observations on the Importance of the American Revolution*, 222, quoted in Greene, *Intellectual Constructions of America*, 139.
164. Raynal, *Revolution in America*, 172-3, quoted in Greene, *Intellectual Construction of America*, 139.
165. Emerson, "The Fortune of the Republic," in *Complete Writings*, 2: 119, quoted in Arieli, *Individualism and Nationalism*, 87.
166. Furay, *Grass-roots Mind in America*, 9.
167. Melville, *White Jacket* (1850), quoted in Prestowitz, *Rouge Nation*, 19.
168. Stephanson, *Manifest Destiny*, 117.

The image has endured right down to the present. Ronald Reagan spoke of America as a "beacon of hope" and "a light unto the nations,"[169] and he predicted her "rendezvous with destiny," a realization of "the last best hope of man on earth."[170]

With regard to feelings of national superiority, the implications of these "light of the world" concepts of the American mission are inescapable. The United States audaciously perceives her cause to be one with that of all humanity. Or as Knud Krakau puts it, "America assumed a vicarious role which gave its actions a meaning that far transcended its boarders" inevitably implicating "nothing less than mankind himself."[171] A disproportionate amount of national rhetoric has been devoted to inspiring fervor for America's universal mission. Again the words of Woodrow Wilson: "The stage is set, the destiny disclosed. America shall in truth show the way.... The light streams upon the path ahead and nowhere else."[172]

Wilson was calling the United States to the moral leadership of the world. Only a nation resolutely certain of its superiority would even consider such a charge. Still, despite the obvious elitist swagger inherent in the idea of America as the "light of the world," there is also an undeniably powerful element of altruism involved. Notwithstanding the inescapable fact of its arrogant, self-righteous assumptions, the genuine benevolence of this American ideal shines through all the pompous notions of its perceived universality. Still, the sad fact remains: no matter how well-meaning the motive, to categorically declare even the most perfected of ideals to be a universal truth, and to stubbornly insist on its universal acceptance, is to tread on very thin ice. Dostoevsky believed that all great nations make this mistake: "Every great people believes and must believe that in it, and it alone, lies the salvation of the world, and that it lives to lead all peoples into the millennium."[173]

STEWARD OF ENLIGHTENMENT

America assumed her messianic role as the secular emancipator of mankind quite naturally. Since the Renaissance, notions of the power and autonomy of the unique individual had been brewing in Europe. Grounded in Classical philosophy, Renaissance humanism preached the dignity and worth of the individual based on the rational ability to determine what is right. This

---

169. Billig, *Banal Nationalism*, 100.
170. Stephanson, *Manifest Destiny*, 127.
171. Krakau, Introduction to *American Nation*, 12.
172. Woodrow Wilson, *Congressional Record*, 66th Congress, 1st Session, 2339, quoted in Weinberg, *Manifest Destiny*, 470.
173. Weinberg, *Manifest Destiny*, 460.

secular intellectual shift was followed by the discovery of the New World in the fifteenth century, the Reformation in the sixteenth and the scientific revolution in the seventeenth. In the wake of it all, the European mind was profoundly altered. At the center of the new patterns of thought was the radical idea that rational thinking, not faith, defined mankind's relation to the world around him. It was the beginning of the Age of Reason, an age in which individual reason became the ultimate measure of "truth, beauty, moral goodness, and political right independent of the dictates of tradition and authority."[174] Mystery and superstition were cast aside, and, like the Christian doctrines that had gone before, the new ideas were embraced as a universal truth. This new truth held that through reason mankind would not only come to understand his world but would also ultimately and inevitably change it for the better, both materially and politically. This is the intellectual core of the Enlightenment and the beginning of the so-called Modern Project of the emancipation of mankind through reason. At the bottom of it all, the Enlightenment fostered the idea that Reason, Freedom, and Progress "naturally imply one another,"[175] and that the West was the birthplace of a universal Enlightenment, which was ultimately to accomplish the salvation of all the peoples of the earth.

Thus, when the American experience began, the mood in Europe was evangelical. Newton was the new Savior, and Locke, Rousseau, Voltaire, and Adam Smith were the new Apostles. The saving truth of the Enlightenment was embodied in a new secular intellectual communion, and America drank heavily of this wine. It was the elixir of revolution. The American children of this sacrament were offspring of the Enlightenment—reason, individualism, liberty, and democracy—and the light that the United States of America was to later hold aloft to the rest of the world was the lamp of Enlightenment —the emancipation of mankind through the application of reason.

As the nineteenth century began, Americans had good reason to feel superior. Their own revolution had met with a political and social success far more radical than that of the English Revolution to which it owed a great debt, and far more enduring than the French Revolution, which had devoured its own children. When, after the French Revolution, Europe again became hopelessly entangled in monarchal wars, in the American mind the torch of Enlightenment progress passed from that continent westward. This is why John Adams viewed the settlement of America as the beginning "the illumination and emancipation of mankind all over the world. "[176] He was speaking not just as an American but also as a voice of the European Enlightenment. In the early years of the republic, the United States saw itself as the only true and legitimately free heir to the

---

174. Cahoone, *Modernism to Postmodernism*, 17.
175. Cahoone, *Modernism to Postmodernism*, 17.
176. John Adams, Notes for "A Dissertation on the Canon and Feudal Law" (1765).

European Age of Reason, and accordingly, America saw a clear duty to bring the Enlightenment to an enslaved world.

The elixir of progress proved headier than the elixir of revolution. In her daze, the new nation saw before it all the progress promised by the Modern Project of Enlightenment. At the same time, she recognized a compelling duty to stand as an example of the emancipation of mankind, demonstrating "enlightened" economic, political, and social success and disseminating an American version of the Universal Truth of the Western Enlightenment. For better or for worse, it is a duty that still calls us.

NOVUS ORDO SECLORUM

In 1802, Noah Webster declared that it had been reserved for America to "discover a great secret."[177] The secret the United States of America would discover was democracy, and America would declare it to the world as a universal truth. It was the unifying principle of the nation's existence. Unlike other nations, which were bound together by ethnicity, culture, and tradition, America was a diverse society, a nation of immigrants. Democracy, not ethnicity, was her national glue. The new nation represented a new way of life and new social order. De Tocqueville grasped the unifying single-mindedness of this idea almost immediately. He quickly came to believe that "in America all laws originated in the same thought: all society rested on a single principle."[178]

In order for an idea to function as a foundation of national identity, national unity, and a platform for national social and political institutions, it must be born of some perceived "ultimate truth or authority, which confers ... absolute validity."[179] In America, democracy was held up as such a notion, and at its side, if not upon its back, where stacked the ideals of liberty, equality, laissez-faire commence, and American individualism. All of this ideology was then neatly wrapped in the enduring notion of providential, divine sanction that had been growing since the Puritans arrived in New England. Thomas Paine had affirmed its universality when he wrote in *Common Sense* that the "cause of America" was "the cause of mankind."[180] To further affirm this national faith, the words "Annuit Coeptis: Novus Ordo Seclorum" were placed on the great seal of the United States. Roughly translated it means, "God has blessed this undertaking: a new order of the ages."

---

177. Noah Webster, "A Oration on the Anniversary of the Declaration of Independence," 1802, quoted in Greene, *Intellectual Construction of America*, 170.
178. Arieli, *Individualism and Nationalism*, 18.
179. Arieli, *Individualism and Nationalism*, 23.
180. Paine, *Complete Writings*, 1:93, quoted in Greene, *Intellectual Construction of America*, 134.

Inherent in all of this was the Enlightenment idea of the natural rights of men, and the growing concept of America as historically elite and therefore separate from the rest of the world. In the early American perspective, independency had been accomplished through the "exertion and bravery of those who left their homes for the sake of civil and religious liberty and in the search of a better life. Having conquered the wilderness by their own unaided exertions, they were masters of their destiny, the sole and lawful possessors of the land, and sovereign makers of their own society."[181] When Jefferson wrote of equality, "inalienable rights," and "the pursuit of happiness," he was not paraphrasing John Locke, he was voicing "native conclusions drawn form the American experience."[182]

This new spirit of independence, together with a passion for liberty and democracy and the inherited "feeling of election to high purpose produced an elevated patriotism which gloried in dreams of destiny."[183] Powerful feelings of national superiority were inescapable. Thomas Paine had sensed this powerful current of American thought when he declared that his newly independent countrymen could "see with other eyes; ... hear with other ears; and think with other thoughts...."[184] Again de Tocqueville saw it clearly in the 1830s:

> Not only are the Anglo-Americans united by their common opinions, but they are separated form all other nations by a feeling of pride. For the last fifty years no pains have been spared to convince the inhabitants of the United States that they are the only religious, enlightened, and free people ... hence they conceive a high opinion of their superiority and are not very remote from believing themselves to be a distinct species of mankind.[185]

Other European observers have noted a similar overt American egoism. The Russian historian I. Dementyev, notes that during the first half of the nineteenth century the United States was "the only large bourgeois republic in the world." According to Dementyev, this along with other features of her political and economic development fueled the enduring American notion that her "political institutions differed fundamentally" from those of Europe."[186] In some substantial part, it was America's unflinchingly negative assessment of European politics and society that had fostered her superior airs from the beginning. De Tocqueville rings in convincingly on this subject as well:

> All nations are vainglorious, but national pride is not displayed by all in the same manner. The Americans, in their intercourse with strangers, appear impatient of the smallest censure and insatiable of the most exhaled praise. The most slender eulogy

---

181. Arieli, *Individualism and Nationalism*, 61-2.
182. Parrinton, *Main Currents*, 1: 194.
183. Arieli, *Individualism and Nationalism*, 62
184. Paine, *Complete Writings*, 1:447, quoted in Greene, *Intellectual Construction of America*, 136.
185. Alexis de Tocqueville, *Democracy in America*, quoted in Stephanson, *Manifest Destiny*, 22.
186. Dementyev, *Imperialist and Anti-Imperialist*, 25.

is acceptable to them, the most exalted seldom contents them; they unceasingly harass you to effort praise, and if you resist their entreaties, they fall to praising themselves.... If I say to an American the country he lives in is a fine one, 'Ay,' he replies, 'there is not its equal in the world.' If I applaud the freedom that its inhabitants enjoy, he answers, 'Freedom is a fine thing, but few nations are worthy of it.' If I remark on the purity of morals that distinguishes the United States, 'I can imagine,' he says, "that a stranger who has witnessed the corruption that prevails in other nations, would be astonished at the difference." At length I leave him to the contemplation of himself; but he returns to the charge and does not desist till he has got me to repeat all that I have been saying.[187]

De Tocqueville's powers of observation are legendary, and as Dementyev points out, the Frenchman was quick to assess "how easily the patriotism of the American, their pride in their social and political institutions, evolved into convictions of their 'superiority.'"[188]Notions of national superiority have occupied the center of the American mind since well before de Tocqueville's time. From the very beginning, American's have been particularly susceptible to visions of "glittering majesty, with virtually every generation regarding itself as chosen by destiny."[189] When Americans invoke the phrase "God Bless America" they are not dedicating the nation to the service of God, they are beseeching God to continue to serve the national order. Such is the arrogance of American democracy.

---

187. Alexis de Tocqueville, *Democracy in America*, Part II, 225, quoted in Dementyev, *Imperialist and Anti-Imperialist*, 25.
188. Dementyev, *Imperialist and Anti-Imperialist*, 25.
189. Furay, *Grass-roots Mind in America*, 7.

CHAPTER 5: IDEOLOGICAL SUPERIORITY

In the 1830s, Alexis de Tocqueville posed a number of questions concerning the success of the "grand American experiment." Perhaps the most penetrating of these was this:

> How does it happen that in the United States, where the inhabitants have only recently immigrated to the land which they now occupy,... [bringing] neither customs nor traditions with them there; where they met one another for the first time with no previous acquaintance; where, in short, the instinctive love of country can scarcely exist ... that everyone takes as zealous an interest in the affairs of his township, his country, and the whole state as it were his own?[190]

In other words, how did this heterogeneous, mobile, and diverse new society hold together as a nation?[191]

De Tocqueville's simple and insightful answer was that democracy lay at the core of American cohesion, but a complete answer is more complex. American was unique. It was not a nation of ethnic, religious, or cultural bonds, nor was it a folk nation unified by a common history or common traditions. America was a nation founded upon an ideal, a nation held together by the adoption of an abstract universal ideology.[192] The fact that America was founded on lofty, universal ideals was what made America unique among nations, fostered her feelings of national superiority, and accounted for American unity. As Richard Hofstadler has famously written, "America *is* an ideology."[193]

---

190. Alexis de Tocqueville, *Democracy in America*, Bradley, ed., 245.

191. Arieli, *Individualism and Nationalism*, 1.

192. Arieli, *Individualism and Nationalism*, 29.

193. Hofstadler, "The Right's Unsung Prophet," in *The Nation*, 248, February 20, 1989, quoted in Lipset, *American Exceptionalism*, 18.

The American people considered themselves a new kind of society governed by a new kind of political order. The very existence of the nation was bound up in new principles of social and political architecture, which had been fashioned using the ideological lumber of natural rights: liberty, equality, and democracy. Out of all of this came the ideology of American individualism, which was wholly unlike any notions of individuality Europe had yet imagined. First the fact of, and later the success of, this ideology, created a kind of national glue and advanced a highly successful socio-political-economic system, which further instilled in America a sense of unity and uniqueness. These convictions combined with a belief in the regenerative power of the new land and a strong sense of chosen-ness, destiny, and universal ideological mission has made it almost impossible for Americans not to feel like superior individuals guiding a superior nation safely across the treacherous shoals of history.

IDEOLOGY AND INFLEXIBILITY

Despite the excellence of American ideals and despite their perceived, broadly humanitarian, universal relevance, there are inherent problems with a nation based on ideology alone. If an ideology is the glue that holds the nation together and the foundation for its society, government, and economy, then ideology is in fact the single key to political and social stability. Thus, the nation will always endeavor to vigorously protect her chosen ideology and reject all others in order to maintain national unity and stability. Other ideologies are necessarily viewed as threats. For this reason, certain aspects of American ideologically developed in a rather fixed way, holding ideological uniformity as a national necessity. Other nations, where the unity of the nation flows from ethnic or cultural uniformity, can tolerate more ideological diversity. In most of the other Western nations, "a variety of ideas may compete with each other." In America, where the basis of national unity is a specific ideology, "diversity can develop only within its [the chosen] ideological framework."[194] America is something of a paradox. Our national ideals allow us the freedom to support any ideology, but since a rather narrow ideological framework holds the nation together, we are unable to fully exercise this freedom without risking harm to the nation itself. Thus, despite undeniable American domestic contributions to social and political progress in the broader world arena of ideas, the United States often fails to "rise above ideology" and continues to "permit dogma to falsify reality, imprison experience, and narrow the spectrum of choice."[195]

---

194. Arieli, *Individualism and Nationalism*, 24.
195. Schlesinger, Jr., "The One Against the Many," in Schlesinger Jr. and White, *Paths of American Thought*, 533.

Yehoshua Arieli contends that "American society can only exist insofar as the individuals of which it is composed carry with them the same ideas and images."[196] Certain ideologies — democracy, liberty, free enterprise — are intrinsically "American" while others –socialism, communism, oligarchy, and theocracy — are, by definition, "un-American." Thus, it is not necessarily that most Americans intellectually oppose socialistic or even communistic ideals, it is that these ideas are antithetical to the fact of America itself, and therefore must be opposed if the nation is to endure.

This makes for a rather restricted national vision. As Arieli puts it, "A multi-national development in most countries of the Western World stimulated understanding of social and political systems differing from their own. The identification of an ideological attitude with America's national interests and aspirations has, on the other hand, made for a strangely unrealistic attitude toward the world at large and toward its own basic problems."[197]

In *Ideology and US Foreign Policy*, Michael Hunt warns that tying our foreign policy to our nationalist ideology exacts a heavy price, perpetuating, "an anxious if not uncomprehending relationship with cultures markedly different from our own, and a misplaced fear of revolutionary change boarding on paranoia."[198] One of America's egoisms is that she is unable to imagine that, just as the United States as a nation is defined by her ideology, other nations may be defined by theirs. The result could be, as Liah Greenfeld warns, "that democracy may not [always] be exportable. It may be an inherent predisposition in certain nations ... yet entirely alien to others."[99] The United States must face the fact that, in some nations, the development of democracy may require nothing less than a complete change of the subject nation's national identity. Thus, unless dominant internal factions desire it, such a change generally requires a brainwashing well beyond the capability of even the most powerful of nations.

IMMIGRANTS AND IDEOLOGY

Proclaiming ideological universality from the very beginning, America opened her ideology to all. As the dispossessed of the world poured in to embrace it, the very fact of such an enormous migration constantly reinforced America's claim to her universal mission and to her universal ideals. The uniqueness of the nation is a result of an unprecedented fusion of peoples. They came by the millions, drawn by the growing myths of the new land: opportunity, freedom, wealth, equality under the law, religious autonomy. Once acquainted

---

196. Arieli, *Individualism and Nationalism*, 3.
197. Arieli, *Individualism and Nationalism*, 20.
198. Hunt, *Ideology and US Foreign Policy*, 192.
199. Greenfeld, *Nationalism*, 10.

with the emerging America ideology of democracy, the sovereignty of the people, social equality, personal liberty, and laissez-faire capitalism, by and large they became zealous converts clinging to a kind of American ideological mysticism in a way that only immigrants fleeing persecution, poverty, and oppression (and finding freedom) could so enthusiastically embrace. America was a nation of immigrants, and as they poured in, they constantly re-confirmed the validity of the ideology upon which the new nation was being built. "The scale and persistence of immigration reassured Americans in the superiority of their society, ... in their moral perfection."[200]

America's national mythology waxes eloquent on the subject of immigration, describing the United States as a great "melting pot" employed "to fuse the characteristics of all peoples into a new and unique metal, to pour it into the mold of the American environment and temper it with American ideas."[201] One historian has called American immigration "the most extensive experiment of the sort since the barbarian invasions of Rome."[202] Indeed, America is defined, in large part, by her complex racial and cultural inheritance, embracing a common ideology in a common environment.

While Americans bristle with pride when they contemplate their benevolence in opening their national arms to "huddled masses yearning to be free," at the same time, many bristle with xenophobic fear in contemplation of the social, political, and religious threats these masses might pose to America's "native" culture. This tension between welcome and rejection constitutes one of the many paradoxes of the American experience. Although America is undoubtedly the world's most successful immigrant experiment, our history overflows with accounts of efforts to limit naturalization in order to maintain political, religious, and ethnic control.[203]

This kind of xenophobia is endemic in most societies. The initial core of American colonization was English, and it is from the English that the United States inherited her original fears of "foreign" cultural pollution. In the beginning, these Anglo-Saxon, Protestant American fears centered on Germans, Scotch-Irish, French Huguenots, and on Roman Catholics and Jews of all nationalities. These fears fostered two types of anti-immigration movements: those aimed at controlling the power of the immigrants admitted, and those aimed at limiting the numbers and kinds of immigrants admitted.[204]

The record of early Anglo-Saxon American xenophobia is clear. Even the great Benjamin Franklin lashed out against German immigrants in Pennsylvania, "Why should the Palatine Boors be suffered to swarm into our settlements, and

---

200. Greenfeld, "American Nationalism," in Krakau, *American Nation*, 37.

201. Morison and Commager, *Growth of the American Republic*, 2: 175.

202. Morison and Commager, *Growth of the American Republic*, 2: 175.

203. Curran, *Xenophobia and Immigration*, 11.

204. Curran, *Xenophobia and Immigration*, 22-3.

herding together, establish their language and manners to the exclusion of ours. Why should Pennsylvania, founded by the English, become a colony of aliens who will shortly be so numerous as to Germanize us instead of Anglifying them."[205]

Despite such sentiments, as long as this remained a rural nation of farmers possessing the seemingly endless free lands of the frontier, assimilation of large numbers of immigrants was accomplished with relative ease. As Crevecoeur, the Frenchman become American-farmer, so eloquently relates, America was a place for strangers to make a new start. Here, Crevecoeur writes, "the idle may be employed, the useless become useful, and the poor become rich; by rich I do not mean gold and silver, we have little of those metals; I mean a better sort of wealth, cleared lands, cattle, food, houses, good clothes, and an increase of people to enjoy them." Here was Jefferson's ideal democratic citizen, the yeoman farmer.

However, with the appearance of great industrial cities with their teeming pockets of foreign-born workers, assimilation became more difficult and native-born resistance grew. Referring to the Irish Catholics in 1844, the *New York American Republican* declared, "... so filthy and ignorant a mass of humanity we have never seen on the face of the earth as is congregated in the cargoes of two to ten or eleven hundred men women and children."[206] By the middle of the 19th century, the cry was heard almost everywhere for a limit immigration, especially Catholic immigration.

Certainly, the case against Catholics ran deeper than just the education and hygiene of arriving Irish, or later of arriving Southern European Roman Catholics. Religious discrimination was quickly turned political, and fears of "Catholic conspiracies" became wide-spread. The centralized control and discipline of the Roman Catholic Church and its refusal to compromise with the ideologies of modernism and nationalism appeared to many Protestants to run sharply counter to the national ideology of secularism and individualism. This is to say, it was feared that Catholicism was by nature un-American. Focusing on the papacy, such fears prompted the "blundering antics of the American Protective Association" in the 1890s and later the revival of the Ku Klux Klan, [207] which cast International Jewry and foreigners of all ethnic backgrounds in a similar conspiratorial light. Although anti-immigration movements have not consistently been in the main current of American thought, they have represented a substantial political force, and in the peak of their fearful frenzies, they accomplished restrictive immigration legislation first in the 1880s and again in the 1920s.

---

205. Benjamin Franklin quoted in Curran, *Xenophobia and Immigration*, 16.
206. Curran, *Xenophobia and Immigration*, 36.
207. Commager, *American Mind*, 191.

As the 19th century ended, singularly vile animosity was displayed toward the Indo-European, Latino, and Chinese foreign-born. The words of Californian governor, Leland Stanford, supply typical example, "There can be no doubt but that the presence of a degraded and distinct people must exercise a deleterious influence upon the superior race."

Such rhetoric reveals an unlovely, eminently self-superior side of the American immigration epic: racism. The founding white Anglo-Saxon Protestant American majority had inherited notions of ethnic superiority from the mother-country. To be sure, this legacy ran contrary to professed core American ideology; nonetheless the undercurrent persisted and as the number of immigrants grew and their ethnic origin strayed farther from Northwestern Europe, racism could be seen in clear relief. From the very beginning, in immigration policy as well as in foreign policy, the United States has ordered humanity according to a well-defined racial hierarchy organized on the principle of skin color, from light to dark, superior to inferior.[208] Today, the test of skin color has fallen from fashion, and the language of "culture" and "development" has replaced the language of race. However, the result is the same.

Despite Anglo-Saxon notions of superiority, despite American native-born political, economic, and social insecurity, despite cultural and religious fears of alien engulfment, the immigrant in America has emerged triumphant. The triumph of the American immigrant experience was due largely to the overwhelming success of the American middle class, which in putting an end to the indigenous American aristocracy, "greatly accelerated the drift toward social uniformity, substituted crude for gracious social standards, and gave to class antipathies an economical rather than a social thrust."[209] Whereas the immigrant masses of the turn of the century may have encountered barriers to immediate and complete Americanization, in large part, the children and grandchildren of these throngs have been welcomed and comfortably seated at the great table of abundance that today feeds the enormous American middle class.

In the shadow of such a triumph, most of the native objections to immigration have proved groundless. It does not appear that the introduction of foreigners upset the equilibrium of the American population. Nor does it appear that immigrants were any less intelligent politically than earlier stock or any less faithful to democracy. The notion that the foreign-born figure more prominently in the spread of crime and disease has also proved to be mythical. As the noted historians Samuel Eliot Morison and Henry Steele Commager put it, "the repeated charge that the immigrant unduly exploited this country loses sight of the extent to which he himself has been exploited, and of his indispensable contribution to developing ... the nation."[210]

---

208. Hunt, *Ideology and US Foreign Policy*, 78-9.
209. Commager, *American Mind*, 46.

It is a sad chapter in the history of the United States that recounts the opposition of "patriotic groups" to a foreign-born presence. Such opposition often included efforts to suppress the cultures, heritages, and traditions of immigrants that otherwise might have added flavor and richness to American life. In the end, the "extreme and often touching eagerness of newcomers to abandon their Old World loyalties and profess those of the New World" proved to be "one of the most striking characteristics of the whole immigration movement."[211] The triumph of the American immigrant experience was a direct result of the migrant's willingness to embrace American ideology, an embrace that often proved stronger than that of the native-born.

For Europeans in the last half of the 19th and early 20th century, America appeared to be an earthly paradise, a model society. When they compared life in their former homelands to the American experience, the result was often a highly polarized, black and white image. To the immigrant of this era, the United States "symbolized freedom, opportunity, and peace; on the other hand, Europe represented suppression, poverty, and war."[212] "In leaving his own country, he asserted his belief in the superiority of the United States."[213] Even if he failed to find all that he dreamed of, he tended to suppress the disappointment in the shadow of the bright, hopeful American myth of regeneration and opportunity. Every new immigrant rushed to grasp at opportunities that had not existed for him in the Old World: land and wealth, social standing and civic participation. In doing so, each immigrant endeavored to make America his own, to be "100% American," and to personally affirm American ideology. The result was a kind of blind nationalism unknown in Europe, the deep national commitment that Leroy Rieselbach calls American "hyper-patriotism."[214] In large part, this kind of immigrant patriotism continues today.

INDIVIDUALISM, IDEOLOGY, AND AMERICAN EXCEPTIONALISM

A great deal has been written about the American notion of individualism. For our purposes, let us define it as the notion that the interests of the individual are paramount, and that individual autonomy must be maintained through liberties of initiative, thought, and action. With such lofty libertarian foundations, individualism itself might be considered an ideology. In America the concept of individualism was a blended product of Enlightenment natural rights theory, a

---

210. Morison and Commager, *Growth of the American Republic*, 2:175-6.
211. Morison and Commager, *Growth of the American Republic*, 2:182.
212. Powaski, *Toward an Entangling Alliance*, xx.
213. Cunliffe, "European Images of America," in Schlesinger Jr. and White, *Paths of American Thought*, 494-5.
214. Rieselbach, *Roots of Isolationism*, 24-5.

belief in the perfectibility of man, and frontier self-reliance, all incorporated into traditionally American social, political, and economic ideologies including democracy, the sovereignty of the people, liberty, equality, free enterprise, and laissez-faire capitalism. For Americans, the resulting amalgam was stronger than the sum of its parts, a sort of "faith," a given, an ingrained truth called individualism, a principle that came to lie at the core of American life.

As the American experience unfolded, individualism became deeply embedded in the culture of the new nation. It existed without proof or opposition. It needed no rationale or defense. Inherent in this "faith" was the idea that the people were sovereign in their power to determine the personnel, structure and policy of the state.[215] John Taylor of Caroline asserted that individualism was voiced in the sovereignty of the people, which "flows from each man's natural right to govern himself."[216]

Although the term is European, individualism in America meant something quite different from individualism in Europe. European individualism was more akin to "individuality." In Europe individualism was bad, synonymous with "selfish," social anarchy, and individual self-assertion, a kind of non-conformity that could threaten the stability of government. In America, it was good, a sort of positive rebellion characterized by an almost unanimous fear of the power of government. In America, individuals acted to carefully limit and specifically define state prerogatives, holding that the common good could be best achieved when each individual was left free to peruse his own self-interest. The political ideas of John Locke, the economic ideas of Adam Smith, and later the anthropological and social ideas that flowed from the writings of Charles Darwin all supported this notion and added to America's all-encompassing ideology of individualism.

Yehoshua Arieli writes that individualism attempted to define the ideals of American life in a generic way:

> Individualism supplied the nation with a rationalization of its characteristic attitudes, behavior patterns and aspirations. It endowed the past, the present and the future with the perspective of unity and progress. It explained the peculiar social and political organization of the nation — unity in spite of heterogeneity — and it pointed toward an ideal of social organization in harmony with American experience. Above all individualism expressed the universalism and idealism most characteristic of the national consciousness.... This two fold aspect — universalism and the capacity to describe values peculiar to American society — made individualism a term synonymous with Americanism.[217]

---

215. Arieli, *Individualism and Nationalism*, 180.
216. John Taylor, *Inquiry into the Principles and Policies of the Government of the United States*, quoted in Arieli, *Individualism and Nationalism*, 171.
217. Arieli, *Individualism and Nationalism*, 186-7.

The American concept of individualism contains not only the roots of American exceptionalism, but also inescapable implications of national superiority. Historian Albert Weinberg, called it, "[America's] blessed egoism in its affirmation of a natural right to the pursuit of happiness."[218] The hardships of colonial life, the settling of the western wilderness, and the revolutionary struggle itself all intensified and further defined American individualism. Hand in hand with these character-building national exertions went a natural feeling of pride, which was evoked by the notion that individualism was American's "choicest, ... peculiar and exclusive possession."[219] As the idea developed, Americans came to view their democracy as the final stage in the development of mankind. According to an 1893 article in the *Democratic Review*, "The course of civilization is the progress of man from the stage of savage individualism to that of an individualism more elevated, moral, and refined."[220]

As Arieli puts it, "Instead of signifying a period of transition toward a higher level of social harmony and unity, it [American individualism] came to mean the final stage of human progress."[221]

Although a sober assessment of America's achievements toward human progress will surly prove a bit more modest, virtually every student of American exceptionalism—that is to say everyone who has asked the question, "Is American Different?"—eventually returns to individualism as the key differentiating factor separating America from the other developed nations of the world. The literature of American exceptionalism is the story of individualism and its interaction with the nation's political, social, economic, and religious ideologies and institutions.

In his study of American exceptionalism, Peter Temin points to the abundance of free land in America that in turn freed labor from the grip of large landowners. According to Temin, this unique economic circumstance along with the spirit of individualism and ingenuity accounted for the growth of the American System and in turn for the later success of American manufacturing.[222] The continuing American "economic miracle" was perpetuated by the fact that, as Seymour Lipset puts it, "From the Revolution on, the United States was a laissez-faire country par excellence."[223] The American popular insistence on governmental protections for "natural" market mechanisms was surely rooted in "rugged individualism." As Byron Shafer writes:

---

218. Weinberg, *Manifest Destiny*, 125.
219. Arieli, *Individualism and Nationalism*, 164.
220. "The Course of Civilization," in US *Magazine and Democratic Review*, 6:209 (1839), quoted in Arieli, *Individualism and Nationalism*, 187.
221. Arieli, *Individualism and Nationalism*, 188-9.
222. Temin, "Free Land and Federalism," 71-93.
223. Lipset, "American Exceptionalism Reaffirmed," 15.

The roots of this are painfully familiar. A nation peopled by originally diverse groups, often dissidents, was to grow by internal migration and external immigration, making collectivism a very difficult [and unlikely] personal orientation, and reinforcing the decentralized and autonomous economic activity which, in turn, further reinforced individualism. More critically, this same symbiotic relationship was to continue over time. The individualism intrinsic to a mercantile and, especially, agriculture economy of the late eighteenth century and early nineteenth centuries was thus to become the individualism intrinsic to the emerging industrial economy and the late nineteenth and early twentieth century, and ultimately the individualism intrinsic to the increasingly post-industrial economy of the late twentieth and early twenty-first centuries. At each point, the individual as a partially autonomous economic unit was necessarily central to an evolving economy, just as the economy found ways of transferring this individualism into new economic [and social] contexts.[224]

The true source of American exceptionalism according to Aaron Wildavsky is not individualism alone, but the way in which individualism reacted to and intermingled with America's evolving ideologies and institutions. Specifically, Wildavsky points to what he perceives to be America's unique ability to reconcile the seemingly irreconcilable tensions between liberty and equality; or as Wildavsky puts it, "What makes America special is the deeply embedded belief, accompanied by supporting institutions, that liberty and equality, the cultures of individualism and egalitarianism, are [or can be] mutually reinforcing."[225] Any nation that can achieve such a feat certainly deserves to be deemed superior; however there is room for considerable debate as to whether, and to what extent, the United States has achieved such a lofty goal.

Inherent in Wildavsky's theory is the notion of the natural, self-regulating mechanisms that Americans first found so attractive in the ideas of John Locke and Adams Smith—the idea that, given a free environment, each individual pursuing his own perceived best interest will work to achieve the larger common good. As Wildavsky puts it, "Where in other Western democracies egalitarians ally with hierarchy to reduce inequality, in America egalitarians have historically allied themselves with individualism."[226] The reason for this was that American egalitarians feared the government as a potential source of inequality and sought to limit its power. Like the libertarians, they saw the spread of individual liberty and the broadening of the individual property-owning base as essential to the defense of their efforts to hold the government in check.

This relates to what Daniel Bell has termed American "civil society," the concept around which he builds his case for American exceptionalism. According to Bell, individualism in America is in constant opposition to hierarchal authority including governmental attempts to impose an egalitarian

---

224. Shafer, "What is the American Way?" 243.
225. Wildavsky, "Individualism and Egalitarianism," 118-9.
226. Wildavsky, "Individualism and Egalitarianism," 119.

society. In America, the role of social leveler, if there was to be one at all, was assigned to economics. As Bell puts it:

> Thus we find a society deeply individualist and populist, its fluid modernity shaped by the open expanse of geography [a natural world that could easily be plundered without remorse] and the economy, by the rule of money, the riches going to the rugged men bent on pursuing their own ends. Both the environment and the economy were unencumbered by polity.... Freedom was defined principally in individualistic economic terms.[227]

In Bell's view of American exceptionalism, the leveling role of government is generally limited to keeping the playing field uniform for business and to facilitating equal opportunity. The true equalizing mechanism is economic, and equalization results in social not necessarily material leveling. As Aaron Wildavsky puts it, "American is about possibilities, not certainties.... Here class divisions do exist but they don't have to matter. Because, in America, competition can be compatible with equality, there is the promise of classlessness."[228]

The question for American exceptionalism today involves an assessment of the present state of both American individualism and equal opportunity. How fares American individualism now that the frontier and free land are long-gone, now that boundless natural resources are no longer there for the more ambitious to exploit, now that the conformity and consumerism of the post-industrial world have weakened the individualist's resolve? And just how equal is opportunity in America? After all, at its most successful, equal opportunity in America was never equality. It was the promise that despite inequalities of all sorts, advancement was still possible, a promise that seems to many today to be a great distance indeed from any claim of reconciling liberty and equality. In America, they will argue, liberty has always held the upper hand over equality.

Whatever the case, it does appear, at least to some significant extent, that individualism and something more like the myth of equality have served to mitigate class conflict in America. This alone might be enough to declare America exceptional or even superior. However, the absence of conflict does not necessarily point to an ongoing balance between liberty and equality. Still, many Americans believe that such a balance has been (or can be) achieved in the United States, and commendably the nation's institutions often reflect this belief.

Still the fact remains, American ideals of liberty and equality are very different from American realities of liberty and equality. Americans have often dedicated themselves to lofty moral propositions that they have later failed to faithfully pursue. American individualism, which lies at the core of the American capitalistic ethos, has its own unique notion of equality, and the national enthusiasm for pure egalitarianism has certainly been "more rhetorical than experi-

---

227. Bell, "The 'Hagelian Secret,'" 65-6.
228. Wildavsky, "Individualism and Equalitarianism," 128.

mental," more mythical than real. The myth of American equality assumes a classless, meritocratic nation, where all individuals are free to pursue material success. This myth creates stability and consensus, and it will persist as long as American abundance provides sufficient evidence pointing to the possibility that it is true. However, whether or not our belief in American equality is rooted in reality, or even in possibility, is not the question here, for the mere belief that America has balanced the scales of liberty and equality is itself enough to give rise not only to political, social, and economic stability but also to strong feelings national superiority.

CHAPTER 6: THE ARROGANCE OF ABUNDANCE

LIBERTY, EQUALITY, AND PROPERTY

The connection between liberty, equality, and property is deeply rooted in the American mind. Writing in the 1830s, de Tocqueville noted the already well-establish linkage. Americans had derived their "love of equality and freedom" from their ancestors dating all the way back to the New World's earliest settlers, "but God himself," de Tocqueville wrote, "gave them the means of remaining equal and free by placing them upon a boundless continent."[229] In *People of Plenty* de Tocqueville's observations became David Potter's theme. According to Potter, American abundance has enabled democratic potential in America.[230]

As the American experience unfolded, notions of national superiority were attached to both the natural abundance of the new land and to what was perceived as a uniquely American ability to exploit this abundance. Notions of American exceptionalism sprang from the belief that the nation could amass material wealth while, at the same time and without contradiction, nurturing her lofty ideology. In fact, material wealth became a measure of the success of that ideology. As de Tocqueville notes, Puritan notions of chosen-ness and divine mission in a New Canaan were reinforced by what appeared to be a grand display of God's favor manifest in the bounty of the land and in the prideful perception of a uniquely American God-given gift for its exploitation.

However, the Puritan seeds planted in the New World yielded a great deal more than just national visions of divinely sanctioned mission and destiny. The Puritan ethos predisposed Americans to notions of both moralism and individu-

---

229. de Toqueville, *Democracy in America*, quoted in Gutfeld, *American Exceptionalism*, 41.
230. Potter, *People of Plenty*, 158.

alism,[231] buttressed the spirit of materialism, and set the tone for American democracy. Since most Puritan sects were congregational, they rejected a hierarchal organization of both church and state. As de Tocqueville noted, Puritanism contained not only a religious doctrine, it also "corresponded in many points with the most absolute democratic and republican theories."[232] Put another way, American Puritanism was the birthplace of egalitarian, individualistic, and populist values that were anti-elitist.[233]

In tandem with, and complimentary to, this liberal polity, American Puritanism exhibited a strong materialistic side. In *American Exceptionalism*, Seymour Lipset points to Max Weber's famous work, *The Protestant Ethic and the Spirit of Capitalism*, noting that the Protestant ethic with its emphasis on the individual, "reinforced values conducive to rational, competitive, individualistic behavior which encouraged entrepreneurial success."[234] According to Lipset and others, American Puritanism carried such ideas to extremes. John Wesley's words supply resounding example. Wesley exhorted "all Christians to gain all they can, and save all they can; that is, in effect to grow rich."[235] America is still taking Wesley's advice, and the national tendency has been to judge other nations using a materialist yardstick.

In his study of American exceptionalism, Arnon Gutfeld offers a more penetrating analysis of the Puritan's materialistic influence on the American ethos. In the Puritan experience, Gutfeld sees a mission dedicated to both perfection and progress. The Puritans believed it their destiny to realize God's kingdom on earth and fancied that they had received unlimited divine license. Since they believed that any success, public or private, enabled this destiny and hastened the kingdom, "Puritan conformism demanded that individuals would devote themselves to constant [economic] improvement." Inherent in this idea was both the notion of constant progress and the creation of a lasting consensus based on the fact that through such progress the Puritans mission satisfied both collective and individual needs. In short, they sought to reconcile the demands of the state with the needs of the individual. The essence of this reconciliation was passed on to the American culture at large in the form of a rhetoric and a mission that could at once encourage materialist free enterprise and maintain unflagging support for liberal polity, all bound up in the notion of "Americanism."[236] A "mission so broad in its implication" according to Sacvan Bercovitch, "that it could facilitate the transition from Puritan to Yankee, and from the (Puritan) errand to manifest destiny and the (American) dream."[237]

---

231. Edmund Burke, *Selected Works*, 180-1, quoted in Lipset, *American Exceptionalism*, 60.
232. Toqueville, *Democracy in America*, 1:36, quoted in Lipset, *American Exceptionalism*, 61.
233. Lipset, *American Exceptionalism*, 61.
234. Lipset, *American Exceptionalism*, 60.
235. Weber, *Protestant Ethic*, 55-6, quoted in Lipset, *American Exceptionalism*, 60.
236. Gutfeld, *American Exceptionalism*, 58.

No one has summarized the Puritan influence in America more eloquently or more exactly than Vernon Parrington:

> In inculcating the doctrine of a sacred calling to work, it substituted the modern attitude towards production for the medieval. It rejected the older conception of work for the sake of livelihood, or production for consumption, and substituted the ideal of work for its own sake, of production for the sake of profit. It implicitly condemned the leisurely, play-loving and pleasure-taking activities of medieval England, and substituted a drab ideal of laborious gain, that measured life in terms of material prosperity and exalted the business of acquisition as the rational end of life. In the sanction of such ethics, wealth became the first object of social desire; and this ideal, that answered the ambitions of the rising middle-class, was preached under the authority of religion. To labor diligently in the vocation to which one is called of God, it was believed, was to labor under the great Taskmaster's eye, and in the confident hope of eternal reward.
>
> No conceivable discipline was better cultivated to breed a utilitarian race....[238]

As usual Parrington captures the raw essence of America: work, money, God. Even in the narrow Puritan experience, whether through the progress of the individual or the furtherance of its collective "errand," the broader mission of American free enterprise was clearly the accumulation of property, and thanks to the Puritan legacy, property in America had assumed a "sacred dimension," it was God-given.[239] Paraphrasing Patricia Limerick, Seymour Lipset puts this legacy in historical perspective. "The most important moral command as perceived by most Americans," he writes in *American Exceptionalism*, "was the accumulation of property."[240]

In the American mind, this national fascination with property and the freedom to pursue it, further set America apart from Europe. European observers of the 1770s and 1780s were quick to seize on the differentiating trend, and the increasingly unique economic character of the American worker. Typical of European observers of the day, is the Englishman Thomas Pownall, who wrote extensively regarding the conditions of labor in the New World as compared to the Old. Pownall's comparisons are stark. For centuries in the Old World, he wrote, labor consisted of "wretches annexed to, but not owner of, the soil; degraded animals that were, as cattle of the field, property not proprietors. They had no interest in their own persons, none in their own labour, none in the produce, either of the earth or of their labour." For Pownall at the time of the American Revolution, labor in Europe could hope for little more than "subsistence and rest." By contrast, Pownall paints labor's lot in America as exactly the opposite. With plenty of land and relatively high wages, he writes, "Every Inhabitant of America" was "his own master both in reasoning and acting; so far as

---

237. Bercovitch, *Rites of Assent*, 35, quoted in Lipset, *American Exceptionalism*, 58.
238. Parrington, *Main Currents*, 1:272.
239. Gutfeld, *American Exceptionalism*, xiii.
240. Limerick, *Legacy of Conquest*, cited in Lipset, *American Exceptionalism*, 20.

respects the individual, he is at perfect liberty to apply his power as he likes, to labour in any line, and to possess and use his property as his own. His property is free from any tenure or condition that may clog, obstruct, or divert the fruits of that labour which he hath mixt with it."[241]

Thomas Pownall understood that the circumstance of labor in America was tied to the intellectual and political climate he found there. In a nation where every man has "the full and free exertion of his powers" and where every man may "acquire any share of the good things thereof," every man could rise to "that natural importance in the Community, which his ingenuity and his manual labour, or his improvements in his landed Property, must of course, unobstructed, give him." In short, Pownall concludes that in America the freedom to work was married to the freedom to rise socially. At the same, time he asserted that Americans, "accustomed to being master of their own property, could never permit anyone to 'assume the power of directing them' in their public affairs."[242]

With property rights thus at the forefront of the young America mind, it can be no coincidence that the framers of the United States Constitution seized on the ideas of John Locke and Adam Smith regarding property. For Locke, the primary end of government was to protect private property, and in asserting the sacredness of property, Locke laid the foundation for capitalism.[243] Smith, with this doctrine of laissez-faire, sought to free economic ambitions from governmental interference. Although in 1776 the leaders of the American Revolution had realized that the war for independence had to be fought on libertarian, philosophical, and ideological grounds in order to muster broad popular support, by the time the Congress met to consider a new constitution in 1787, a remarkable change had taken place. The framers of the Constitution put aside the lofty liberal ideals that had served them so well in the fight for independence and turned realists. French humanitarian concepts of equality and fraternity found little response in an America again concerned with the accumulation and protection of property. As Parrington puts it, "The revolutionary concept of equalitarianism, that asserted the rights of man apart from property and superior to property, did not enter into their thinking."[244]

Beginning with the very first settlers, Americans had considered it their sacred calling to reap the abundant harvest of their bountiful new land. The United States Constitution sought to establish their right to do exactly that. The founders did not intend to guarantee absolute social equality, but rather to protect property and insure the social and economic elasticity necessary to

---

241. Pownall, *Memorial to the Sovereigns of Europe*, 42-3, 48-9; Pownall, *Memorial to the Sovereigns of America*, 54-6, quoted in Greene, *Intellectual Construction of America*, 145-6.
242. Pownall, *Memorial to the Sovereigns of America*, 42-5, quoted in Greene, *Intellectual Construction of America*, 147.
243. Parrington, *Main Currents*, 1:274.
244. Parrington, *Main Currents*, 1:286.

create broad opportunities for sharing in the harvest of America's abundance. As a result of this distinctly economic Constitutional orientation, American social and economic institutions have developed in a unique way. The result has been unprecedented political stability. Up until the last few decades, tension between workers and the wealthy and powerful has been largely negated in the United States by the worker's own aspirations to become wealthy and powerful. As Gutfeld puts it, American workers see themselves as "potential capitalists." According to Gutfeld, the social battle in the United States has not been between the "haves" and the "have-nots" but between the "haves" and the self-styled "will-haves." In this context, the majority of American workers have historically perceived any attack on laissez-faire capitalism not only to be an attack on American freedoms, but also a direct attack on their individual chances for success.[245]

In the shadow of such a stabilizing social force, and despite recessions, depressions, and cycles of economic ebb and flow, real income in America has steadily increased, thus adding to the stability of the system. In addition, growing confidence in the opportunity for advancement has made it possible to assimilate enormous immigrant populations into the United States without significant destabilizing effect. Finally, long-term economic growth and the continuing prospects for equality created by the enduring perception of all-embracing freedom of opportunity have created a prideful national belief in American progress. Our history as a nation has instilled in us the dangerous and arrogant fantasy that every new generation will be materially better off than the generation before it.

THE TRIUMPH OF LAISSEZ-FAIRE

A hundred years after the ratification of the Constitution, the framers would have been hard pressed to recognize the nation they had created. The protections they had built into the Constitution had afforded Americans limitless prospects for exploitation, which gathered in all the old Puritan restraints and inhibitions, eclipsed the idealism of Jefferson and ignored the reforming spirit of Jackson. The end of the Civil War announced the decline of agricultural America and declared industrial America ascendant, and the nation set about the business of making money. It was as if the original Puritan epic and later the hardships of frontier life had instilled in the nation a great store of pent up material desires, which the Gilded Age released. As the nineteenth century drew to a close, Parrington describes an America "consumed with a hunger for abundance." He writes of "freedom and opportunity, to acquire, to possess, to enjoy."

---

245. Gutfeld, *American Exceptionalism*, xvi.

For that, he concludes, the nation "would sell her soul."[246] Freedom became individualism, and individualism became the right to preempt, to exploit, to squander.[247] Out of this crude energy, the sprawling American middle class materialized, politically dominant, dedicated to capitalism, and bolstered by the triumph of America's blossoming laissez-faire economy.[248] Within half a century, it would give a new meaning to American abundance by creating the greatest industrial order on earth.

In the American mind, the triumph of laissez-faire in the last decades of the nineteenth century both confirmed and bound together a number of ideas that had been steadfastly believed but only loosely connected. Like the individualism of the frontier, American laissez-faire capitalism in the Gilded Age gathered into its embrace and welded together American notions of liberty, property, social mobility and economic opportunity. Included in laissez-faire's broad embrace were John Locke's concepts regarding the self-regulating natural laws governing free men, who in pursuing individual interests would ultimately further the common good. Indeed, laissez-faire became the living embodiment of Locke's ideal, which remains foundational in the American political mind— Thomas Paine's famous notion of the perfection of the "government that governs least."

At the same time, the ethic of laissez-faire capitalism incorporated and venerated ingrained Puritan notions of hard work, material accumulation, sobriety, persistence, patience, and thrift. All of this "made a strong appeal to the natural optimism of the American people," writes Morton White. "The appeal to the harmonies of a self-regulating economic system was strongly linked with the belief in national as well as individual progress.[249] With what Louis Hacker has called "the triumph of American capitalism,"[250] all of America's traditional political, social, and economic traditions were re-validated in the idea of laissez-faire—an idea that dominated the national imagination, exuded boundless confidence in its own resourcefulness, and ultimately became embedded in the myth and legendry of the American people.[251] At the most fundamental level, laissez faire invokes Adams Smith's famous "invisible hand of competition" a natural mechanism that renders individual decisions collectively congruous with the general good, thus linking American self-reliant individualism to a "higher" order of Nature. It also reinforces American Puritan notions of the tyranny of hierarchal organization and the larger Calvinist belief that individual economic

---

246. Parrington, *Main Currents*, 3:11.
247. Parrington, *Main Currents*, 3:17.
248. Lerner, "The Triumph of Laissez-faire," 149.
249. White, *Social Thought in America*, quoted in Lerner, "The Triumph of Laissez-faire," 155.
250. Hacker, *Triumph of American Capitalism*.
251. Lerner, "The Triumph of Laissez-faire," 150.

success is beneficial to the community at large. Finally, laissez-faire meshes nicely with the Darwinist ideas of Herbert Spencer, ideas that found favor in America in the last decades of the nineteenth century. For Spencer, the idea of conflict and competition in Nature clearly carried over into the realm of the competitive nation and the successful competitive individual. In this view, the idea of natural selection and the survival of the fittest found proof in the success of laissez-faire and the new American economic order.

Despite the fact that laissez-faire is today only a faded relic of its triumphant dominance in late nineteenth century, it still holds sway over part on the American mind. As the appearance of large corporations transformed the American economy, "the idyllic self-regulating society governed only by moral individualism" became "a rationale for the power of business collectivism."[252] In the end, there turned out to be a marked difference between the "perfect competition" of theory and the "imperfect competition" of industrial reality,[253] and as the twentieth century began, the government moved to supply remedy. It has been doing so even since. Nonetheless, the notion of laissez-affair remains deeply engrained in the American consciousness.

In *The Poverty of Affluence*, Paul Wachtel calls laissez-faire free competition America's "official state religion." Like all religions, Wachtel insists, it "plays an essential role in our relationships with others and our sense of ourselves." Also like religion, we expect a great deal from our free competitive system. In the economic world, we expect it to act as a mechanism to insure that we get the goods and services we need, when we need them, and at the best price. In the competitive world of ideas, we expect the truth to win out. The trouble is, according to Wachtel, there are some problems facing us that can not be solved by an "individualistic, competitive market approach." Some problems can not be solved by any of us alone, but require "cooperation and recognition of our shared stake in certain solutions," and, Wachtel warns, "this suggestion runs counter to a deep strain in American life."[254]

Implied in the idea of laissez-faire is a fundamental arrogance. Any idea that claims to take its authority from the Natural order or from God inherently presumes itself superior to opposing ideas taking their authority from the edicts of man. From its perceived origin in "higher law," laissez-faire assumes a providential mission and a providential destiny. In the American mind, a laissez-faire system is the ultimate natural destiny of mankind, a universal truth entrusted to this nation for the ultimate betterment of all of the nations of the world. In addition, it carries with it the affirmation of American notions of the equality of opportunity—notions that are not wholly egalitarian but rather hold that despite our inequalities, the avenues to success are open to all. This notion when

---

252. Lerner, "The Triumph of Laissez-faire," 149.
253. Lerner, "The Triumph of Laissez-faire," 154.
254. Wachtel, *The Poverty of Affluence*, 284-5.

cloaked in garments of laissez-faire gives rise to the idea that this kind of equality means that we all get what we deserve—that the rich rise on their merits and the poor somehow deserve their fate—that those blessed with property have a right to feel superior. A TV advertisement of a few years ago proclaimed, "We make our money the old fashioned way—we *earn* it." Americans found this message compelling, because the idea derives its power from the notion that American wealth comes from hard work and, without saying it, implies that poverty comes from sloth.

At the bottom of it all, lies the uniquely American concept that abundance and ability constitute national and individual manifestations of God's approval accessed through work. Wrapped in the gleaming mantel of laissez-faire and the survival of the fittest, America declares her God-given superiority as confirmed by the fact that she has become the wealthiest nation on earth. What is more, this proclamation is made in the belief that the achievement of her remarkable wealth stands as indisputable God-given proof that the "American Way" is the right way and represents the inevitable destiny of mankind.

THE AMERICAN ECONOMIC MIRACLE

The economic miracle that transformed America into the world's wealthiest nation was so awe-inspiring that most Americans find it difficult to believe that it, like all miracles, was not accomplished by the hand of God. In 1879, the US was still a country of extractive industries, but the last decades of the eighteenth century began what Charles and Mary Beard have called the "Second American Revolution," an explosion of American technology, industry, and change. By the first decades of the twentieth century, the United States had become one of the greatest manufacturing nations in the world.[255] By 1890 American pig iron production had moved ahead of English production; by 1915 American coal production was twice that of England, the former world leader; and by that time America had taken a clear lead in electrical power generation.[256] Even Vladimir Lenin remarked on this nation's miraculous growth, "[t]he USA is unrivaled either in the rate of development of capitalism at the turn of century, or in the record level of capitalist development already obtained," he wrote in 1915.[257] What would have been even more remarkable to Lenin, had he lived to witness it, was the continuing rise in the real wages of the American worker over the span of the twentieth century. By the inter-war years, "the industrial world recognized the United States as the pre-eminent techno-

---

255. Morison, *Oxford History of the American People*, 761.
256. Hughes, *American Genius*, 15.
257. Vladimir Lenin, *Collected Works*, 22:17, quoted in Dementyev, *Imperialist and Anti-imperialist*, 13.

logical nation, and the era of technological enthusiasm reached its apogee,"[258] and as the century progressed, "the American economy provided an example to the world both of aggregate growth with immigration and of managerial forms for corporate economic life."[259] American had good reason to feel superior in this regard. Today the United States, with less than 5% of the world's population, accounts for over 30% of the world's GDP and 25% of world energy consumption (an incredible 100 quadrillion BTUs); US stock markets account for 36% of the equities traded worldwide; and US research and development makes up over 40% of the world total.

In the American mind, success is measured in large part by material wealth, and by this precisely quantifiable yardstick America is indubitably superior to the other nations of the world. The natural grass-roots American reaction to the nation's meteoric material ascendancy is that America must be doing something right, that the national values must be in good order. Conversely, to the extent that American's can bring themselves to believe their dominant economic hegemony to be currently slipping, they instinctively blame an erosion of national values. In the American mind, there is a clear connection between superior material wealth and superior values. We are rewarded when we are good and punished when we are bad. Every child knows that.

Miracles are for the chosen, but Americans are generous with their miracles. The United States still revels in the success of its efforts to rebuild the economies of former enemies after World War II. The economic miracle in Japan has been truly astounding, Germany had her *Wirtschaftswunder*, and Italy had her *miracolo economico*. Later America would proudly point to the South Korean miracle, but she would seldom mention the fact that that nation remained under the rule of string of military dictators for decades after its "liberation." Nonetheless, there is a part of the American mind that still resolutely believes that the benevolent touch of the magic wand of American democracy and laissez-faire capitalism will produce economic, social, and political miracles around the world, whether the "beneficiaries" are willing recipients or not. It is a noble vision by American standards, but it is also naive, and a shameless arrogance by many other measures.

THE MYTH OF AMERICAN TECHNOLOGICAL SUPREMACY

At the confluence of the abundance of the New World and the American economic and industrial miracle lies the myth of American technological supremacy. From the nation's beginnings, Americans have seen themselves as

---

258. Hughes, *American Genius*, 9.
259. Temin, "Free Land and Federalism," 92.

the possessors of a special kind of practical inventiveness and a unique inborn knack for organization and innovation that surpass that of any other nation. This myth is reflected in popular turns of phrase like "Yankee ingenuity" and "American know-how." Such terms suggest a national aptitude for machinery and innovative problem solving. Americans are convinced that their industrial and material successes are due in part to an innate national ability to create and manage technology and business that surpasses that of other nations.

Fundamental to this notion is the idea that Americans are a fiercely practical people, and that American innovations offer real solutions to real problems, not theoretical answers to scientific puzzles. In 1838, the English engineer Thomas Tredgold, writing on the progress of the steam engine, noted American inventiveness, but also noted that that "American technology depended little on science."[260] It was not until the last half of the twentieth century that the myth of the gifted America individual inventor finally migrated to a broader belief in the nation's superior ability to create complex scientific, technological, and managerial systems designed to serve practical ends. In his study of technology in early America, Brooke Hindle puts it nicely, "... at the popular level there is [still] the conflicting image of American whittling boys inventing their way—through cotton gins, steamboats, mass production, telegraphs, and vulcanized rubber—from the colonial world of hand production to the new world of machine production."[261]

As with all American superiority myths, the rationale for perceived national technological and managerial superiority was rooted in ideology. Certainly, it was no coincidence that the Industrial Revolution began at about the same time that America secured her independence from England. The year 1776 saw both a demonstration of James Watts' first successful steam engine and the publication of Adam Smith's *Wealth of Nations*.[262] In the broadest overview, the same spirit of Enlightenment drove the Industrial Revolution, the capitalist economic revolution, and the American Revolution. In the American mind, the spirit of liberty nurtured both the spirit of invention and the success of the nation's entrepreneurial endeavors.

There is some truth in this belief. American notions of liberty and equality bound up in the freedom of opportunity sparked unprecedented individual "activity and industry." According to *Columbia Magazine* in 1786, "The cup is within the reach of every man, full to the brim, but the exertion to take it must be arise from himself."[263] In America, there was a new life to be won, and owing

---

260. Tredgold, *Steam Engine*, 1:43.
261. Hindle, *Technology in Early America*, 19.
262. Hindle, *Emulation and Invention*, 2.
263. "Enquiry into the Most Advantageous Occupations to be Followed by Persons Emigrating to America," in *Columbia Magazine*, October, 1787, 699-700, quoted in Greene, *Intellectual Construction of American*, 176.

to the hardships of the new land, attitudes toward possible solutions were more practical, open, and flexible than in the Old World. Most European accounts of America after the Revolution pointed to the widespread "industry of the people," and many Old World observers noted that Americans were uniquely adaptable. For a nation of isolated farmers, necessity was indeed the mother of invention. In this regard, in 1839 Michael Chevalier wrote that the American conformed "easily to new situations and circumstances; he is always ready to adopt new processes and implements, or to change his occupation. He is a mechanic by nature."[264]

Writing on the progress of American's early railroads in 1836, the Frenchman, Guillaume Tell Poussin captured the connection between American ideology and technology perfectly:

> Steam, with the Americans, is an eminently national element, adapted to their character, their manners, their habits, and their necessities. With them it is applied as much to extend their liberty as to augment their physical welfare.... The American seems to consider the words democracy, liberalism, and railroads as synonymous terms.[265]

Individuals of two types populate the American myth of technological superiority: inventors like Samuel Morse and Thomas Edison and organizers like Henry Ford and Fredrick Taylor. As the American experience unfolded, it became clear that the national technological gift included more than mechanical and electrical problem solving, that it went beyond the creation of so-called inventions. In order to utilize the new inventions, new systems of were needed. As Thomas Hughes observes in *American Genius*, by 1900 the nation had "acquired the traits that have become [are perceived to be] characteristically American, ... a nation of machine makers and system builders ... imbued with a drive for order, system, and control."[266] America was the first nation to fully realize that, in the broader scope of true industrial progress, machines were "mere components in highly organized and controlled technological systems."[267]

This idea first became clear at the beginning of the nineteenth century with the appearance of the American System of Manufacture. Eli Whitney's concept of interchangeable parts implied a great deal more than just an assembly line. It pointed the way to the highly complex, integrated systems of machines, people, organizations, and finance needed to efficiently combine technology, labor, management, procurement, engineering, research, transportation, finance, distribution, and sales—systems that would transform a wilderness into a

---

264. Chevalier, *Society, Manners and Politics*, 285.
265. Poussin, *Chemins de Fer Américains*, xvi; *United States: Its Power and Progress*, 345, 371, quoted in Greene, *Intellectual Construction of America*, 27.
266. Hughes, *American Genius*, 1.
267. Hughes, *American Genius*, 184.

building site and nation of farmers into a nation of industrial workers, clerks, and business men.

In *They Made America*, Harold Evans contends that true American national genius is not solely a gift for invention, but rather a gift for innovation, which he defines as "invention put to use." Cyrus McCormick was not the only farmer to invent the reaper," Evans explains, "but he was the only one who initiated the financing mechanisms that made it possible for hundreds of thousands of farmers to afford the invention." Evan's notions of American innovative genius go beyond simple invention to the forces that propel an invention into widespread use, including the ability to imagine a new invention's use. "Theodore Maiman, having invented the first working laser on May 16, 1960," Evans writes, "described it as 'a solution in search of a problem,' because so few appreciated its manifold possibilities." In defining applications for his product and founding his own companies to exploit these applications, Maiman was an innovator as well as an inventor. The effect of American innovation was thus a kind of democratization that made it possible for the entire population to enjoy goods and services once available only to the privileged few. Evans also notes a distinctly entrepreneurial spirit in all of this—a decidedly altruistic motive that also appeared to be uniquely American.[268]

Propelled by the profit motive and what she perceived to be a national gift for innovation, it took America a little over one hundred years to move from the handful of workers on the first assembly line at the Whitneyville Armory to Henry Ford's massive blast furnaces and assembly plants at Highland Park and River Rouge. Along the way, the myth of technological superiority had broadened into a national belief in a uniquely American gift for organization and scientific management. The notion grew that Americans were not only superior to other national peoples in their mastery of technology but also in their mastery of business—not only better inventors and innovators, but also better organizers, entrepreneurs, and businessmen.

In the American mind, when the United States, with its supreme industrial might, entered the First World war the stalemate was broken. Likewise, in the Second World War even before the development of the atomic bomb, there was little doubt in anyone's mind that the strength and flexibility of the US industrial complex was the key to victory. Thus, in the first half of the twentieth century, America demonstrated her technological and managerial superiority to the world in a concrete way that was a great deal more convincing than the dull statistics of production and industrial efficiency.

In the ongoing American marriage of ideology and technology it was believed that each partner legitimized the other, that America material success was enabled by America virtue, and that national virtue was reflected in the national wealth. After Hiroshima, the inevitable offspring of the marriage

---

268. Evans, *They Made America*, 10-11.

between ideology and weaponry was the conviction that the United States was invincible in war. Certainly, there was nothing new about the idea that there is strength in virtue, and America still proceeds with the memory of World War II remarkably fresh in her national mind. As Loren Baritz puts it speaking of the Viet Nam War, "It was unthinkable that America's military could ever fail to establish its supremacy on the battlefield, that the industrial, scientific, and technological strength of the nation would ever be insufficient for the purposes of war." [269]

However, somewhere along the way, something had gone wrong. Eli Whitney's simple arms assembly line near New Haven had opened the door for the genius of Henry Ford and others create to the mega-industrial complexes that produced motorcars and washing machines that everyone could afford. It was a very American story and a great source of national pride, but the story of America's journey from the Ford Motor Company to the later-day arms assembly line of the Manhattan Project was troubling. Gone were America's "whittling boys," swept up in a maelstrom of technology so deep as to seemingly defy human understanding and engulfed by multifaceted organizations so vast that they appeared to be beyond the control of anyone. With the appearance of the so-called "military industrial complex," the US government and the American mega-industrial culture combined to project American power throughout the world. The Manhattan Project offers a supreme example. Highly technical, rooted in the murky disciplines of "pure theoretical science," advanced not by Americans but by an international array of highly abstract thinkers, and funded secretly by the US government, the Manhattan project resulted in a product that would give America supreme and unquestioned military power in the world. Ironically, the proliferation of this product would soon, in a very real way, render all the nations of the world equal.

The result was the so-called "arms race," a contest that proved America's burning need to confirm the superiority not only of her technology but also of her ideology. As we have seen, the two were powerfully linked in the American mind. America's technology, both for consumption and for destruction, was deemed superior not only because of its abundant success, but also because of the superiority of the national ideology that had enabled and nurtured it in the first place. With the onset of the arms race, US superiority in all areas was suddenly measured not only in GNP and in TV sets and dishwashers designed to benefit individual consumers, but also in warheads and nuclear delivery systems. It was unimaginable that America could fall behind, that she could ever be anything other than "number one," even if the individual was trampled underfoot in the effort.

The history of NASA and the US space program is also instructive in this regard. Begun as a purely scientific offshoot of the American military industrial

---

269. Baritz, "God's Country and American Know-How," 480.

complex, it soon degenerated into the so-called "space race," a contest to prove world technological superiority. America was dumbfounded when the Russians were the first to orbit the earth. It was unthinkable that our technological superiority could be challenged. From the launch of Sputnik until Neil Armstrong walked on the surface of the moon, the driving force behind NASA was the demonstration of unassailable American technological superiority.

With the advent of the global economy, it has slowly become clear that America does not posses any unique inborn technological or managerial gifts that are not given to others. In recent years, Japan and the European Economic Community, along with other nations, have excelled not only in creating new technologies, but also in building the mega-systems needed for their exploitation and dissemination. The fact of this is hard to swallow for Americans and the myth of technological superiority lingers sometimes at the expense of cooperative efforts to serve the best interests of the global population.

Every now and than, a Jonus Salk appears—a free, hardworking, persevering individual, who, seemingly working in isolation, changes the world. This rarely happens any more, but when this does, the American national imagination still soars.

CHAPTER 7: THE ARROGANCE OF ISOLATIONISM

The seeds of isolationism began to germinate very early in the American experience, and they took root, sprouted, and blossomed in the same soil that nurtured American feelings of mission and pre-eminence. In the beginning, the great oceans that surrounded the New World provided isolation enough for the early pioneer colonials, who knew from bitter experience that the Atlantic was rough and hazardous to cross. Early maps depicted the oceans in "surrealistic proportions," as if "God Himself" had intended to separate the "new American Zion" from the corruption of Europe.[270] Independent, self-reliant and increasingly critical of Old World ways, this new breed of men was shaped by both the hardships and the abundance of the great virgin wilderness.

EARLY AMERICAN ISOLATION

Although the early English colonial inhabitants of America first thought of themselves as Englishmen, as the colonies grew, an undercurrent of social and political separateness accompanied budding feelings of superiority. American notions of separateness and superiority sprang from myths of the unique regenerative power of the new land; from visions of chosen-ness, mission and high destiny; from the indelible lessons of frontier self-sufficiency; from the abundance of the great, green continent; from a developing sense of American uniqueness and finally from the perceived universality of the emerging American ideology. A people that believes itself superior to all other peoples, naturally seeks to set itself apart.

---

270. Adler, *Isolationist Impulse*, 9.

The American Revolution was itself an act of isolation, severing ties with the mother country.[271] This schism unleashed a wide-spread desire to hold the emerging new society separate and morally aloof from the rest of the world. Thus, the American War for Independence was a war for independence in a very broad sense of the word. It was not only about freeing America from English imperial abuse; it was also about holding separate and protecting idealistic American social values like liberty and equality; political values like democracy and the sovereignty of the people; and economic values like laissez-faire capitalism.

In the eyes of most American immigrants, Europe was unnecessarily militant, morally decadent, politically reactionary, socially rigid, and economically imperialistic and mercantile. Americans saw themselves as a completely new kind of society, and although they held their new undertaking up as "a light to the world," they nonetheless sought complete separation from the corrupting influence of European decadence and tyranny. In 1795, the American legal theorist, James Kent described European "fetters, entailments, and perpetuities" that "foster excessive inequalities, facilitate corruption, unduly widen distinctions, and humble the poor under the proud superiority of the rich."[272] As Thomas Paine put it, "It is clear they belong to different systems: England to Europe, and America to itself."[273] Yehoshua Arieli sums up early American isolationism's compact rationale:

> ... [G]rowing isolationism derived from the conviction that only an absolute disengagement from diseased and corrupted Europe could safeguard the hard won achievements of the American Republic. The failure of the French Revolution, its embroilment in unceasing wars with monarchal Europe, its final destruction through the forces it had let loose, and the final victory and restoration of a reactionary and tyrannical regime, all these strengthened and fortified to isolate the American continent completely from the remainder of the world and to make it strong, independent and self-sufficient.[274]

The United States Constitution reflected early isolationist sentiment when the framers required a 2/3 vote in Congress to ratify foreign treaties and forbade American officials from accepting foreign offices and titles. It was even suggested that the office of Secretary of State should be temporary.[275] In 1796, George Washington declared, "The great rule of conduct for us in regard to foreign nations is, in extending our commercial relations, to have as little political connection as possible. It is our true policy to steer clear of permanent alliances with any portion of the foreign world."[276] Washington urged American

---

271. Adler, *Isolationist Impulse*, 10.
272. Kent, *Dissertations*, 17-18, quoted in Greene, *Intellectual Construction of America*, 179.
273. Paine, *Writings*, 92.
274. Arieli, *Individualism and Nationalism*, 128.
275. Powaski, *Toward an Entangling Alliance*, xiv.

to take advantage of their "detached and distant situation," although he did recognize "temporary alliances" as potentially useful and safe in "extrodinary emergincies."[277]

Jefferson agreed. He declared that the new nation's "first and fundamental axiom should be never to entangle ourselves in the broils of Europe."[278] In his inaugural address he urged, "honest friendship with all nations, entangling alliances with none."[279] In support of this dictum, he declared America to be "the world's best hope," and observed that the new nation was "kindly separated by nature and a wide ocean from the exterminating havoc of one quarter of the globe; too high-minded to endure the degradations of the others; possessing a chosen country, with room enough for our descendants to the thousandth and thousandth generation."[280] For Jefferson, such superior, self-sufficient, isolationist notions were not mere sentiment. They were based on firm ideological principles. He saw the American continent as a stronghold of liberty, a "signal arousing men to burst the chains under which ignorance and superstition had persuaded them to bind themselves...."[281] Like Washington, Jefferson saw the reality of the American position: "a weak and untried republic, striving to make its mark in a warring, unfriendly and monarchal world." With European colonial empires on all sides, early American leaders prized isolationism because it insured freedom of action "to prevent foreign subversion, and to enable us to take advantage of Europe's distress in order to round out our own boundaries."[282] In part, the Louisiana Purchase was motivated by Jefferson's desire to protect the new nation from European expansion.

Jefferson's writings abound with the rhetoric of isolationism. His opposing images are consistent. America always points to the future cast in the halo of liberty, happiness, innocence, and simplicity. Europe always points toward the past characterized by despotism, misery, corruption, and sophistication. "This dualism became the image that shaped American isolationism for most of the 19th century."[283] For the Jeffersonians, safeguarding republicanism required geographical demarcation, a clear dividing line between American and the rest of the world.[284]

---

276. George Washington, "Farewell Address," quoted in Rieselbach, *Roots of Isolationism*, 9.

277. George Washington, "Farewell Address," quoted in Adler, *Isolationist Impulse*, 11.

278. Thomas Jefferson, *Writings*, 14:43-5.

279. Thomas Jefferson, First Inaugural Address, 1801.

280. Thomas Jefferson, First Inaugural Address, 1801.

281. Thomas Jefferson, letter Roger C. Weightman, June 24, 1826, in *Writings*, 16:182, quoted in Arieli, *Individualism and Nationalism*, 128.

282. Adler, *Isolationist Impulse*, 11.

283. Perkins, *History of the Monroe Doctrine*, xvii.

284. Arieli, *Individualism and Nationalism*, 128-9.

As the nineteenth century unfolded and other national revolutionary movements took up the banner of freedom, American remained aloof, a distant and self-proclaimed guiding light. Despite the fact it was widely believed that her own free institutions and her place in the world would be strengthened by the success of liberty and democracy elsewhere in the world, the United States resisted the temptation to become actively involved in foreign causes, no matter how noble. When in 1821 the heroic stand of Greek patriots against the Turks stirred libertarian emotions in America, Secretary of State John Quincy Adams sought to cool such passions. "[America] goes not abroad in search of monsters to destroy," he wrote. "She is the well-wisher to the freedom and independence of all. She is the champion and vindicator only of her own." Adams warned that intervention would change "the fundamental maxim of her [America's] policy from liberty to force."[285] When Hungarian freedom fighters sought US aid in 1848, Henry Clay admonish that the cause of world liberty would be better served by Americans keeping their "lamp burning brightly on the Western shore, as a light to all nations, than to hazard its utter extinction, amid the ruins of fallen or falling republics in Europe."[286] Certainly, notions of American moral superiority and European decadence ran through all of this.

Americans saw themselves as different. In America, careers were open to talent, the gulf between rich and poor was not so wide as in Europe, and class distinctions were less important. The new nation abounded with new conceptions and new destinies. As historian Dexter Perkins puts it, "From this sense of different-ness, there was bound to flow the notion that the rupture of the ... connection with time-worn Europe ought to be as complete as possible, that non-entanglement was the true basis of American foreign policy."[287]

As the nation grew, isolationism continued to be the guiding principle of American foreign policy, and always at its root was Jefferson's vision of an ideological stronghold. Over time, US isolationism also grew out of the widespread American desire to retain the option of independent or unilateral military action or diplomacy unfettered by alliances. All of this drew popular support from an ingrained, American, nationalist mistrust of foreigners, a burning national sense of individualism and self-sufficiency, and the "hyper-patriotism" of the immigrant mind. The result was an arrogant, nationalist, closed-minded rejection of all things "un-American."[288]

---

285. John Quincy Adams in *Niles Weekly Register*, XX, July 21, 1821, 326, quoted in Adler, *Isolationist Impulse*, 14.

286. Henry Clay quoted in Moore, *American Democracy*, 139, quoted in Adler, *Isolationist Impulse*, 15.

287. Perkins, *History of the Monroe Doctrine*, 5.

288. Rieselbach, *Roots of Isolationism*, 24-5.

THE MONROE DOCTRINE

In 1823, all of this came together in the famous Monroe Doctrine. In it President Monroe declared, "the American continents, by the free and independent condition which they have assumed and maintain, are henceforth not to be considered subject for future colonization by any European power." Monroe went on to declare "any attempt ... to extend their [Europe's] political system to any part of this hemisphere as dangerous to our peace and safety." Manifestly clear in Monroe's language was the fact that America considered her political ideas to be antithetical to European ideals. In short, Europe was governed by absolutist principles and America by the principles of democracy.[289]

The American reaction to Monroe's proclamation was electric. According to a British observer, Monroe had "found a chord which vibrates in strict unison with the sentiments" of the nation.[290] The sentiments, which were so patriotically set to vibrating by the Monroe Doctrine, were the familiar notions of America as "the favorite child of God, Nature, and History."[291] For many Americans, the Monroe Doctrine formally proclaimed America's providential, separateness, strength, and superiority to the entire world. "The isolationist tradition thus acquired a sanctity which inspired a fierce belief, easily transformed into pharisaical righteousness and blind bigotry."[292]

The Monroe Doctrine created an unbridgeable gulf between America and Europe. In America, "The belief was well neigh universal that the United States was so strong, so vigorous, so dynamic — so morally superior — that it could ignore all other countries."[293] By the end of the Civil War, such arrogant visions of national self-sufficiency had become even more grandiose. As the Gilded Age began, notions of American security, superiority, and power were on the rise, fed by the strength of the nation's geographical location, the size of her territory, and the progress of her growing industrial might.[294]

All the while, the great oceans that separated America from the rest of the world worked to circumscribe the American mind. The less one knows of the world, the more alien other cultures will appear and the more one's own culture, traditions, and habits of thought will appear to represent the only true, logical, and correct interpretation of human experience. This kind of thinking represents a solipsism, a theory that holds up the self as the only existing thing—a belief that one's self is the world—that "they are us," or at least that they want to

---

289. Perkins, *History of the Monroe Doctrine*, 63.
290. Perkins, *History of the Monroe Doctrine*, 62-3.
291. Powaski, *History of the Monroe Doctrine*, xix.
292. Powaski, *Toward an Entangling Alliance*, xix.
293. Foster Rhea Dulles, *America's Rise to Power*, quoted in Powaski, *Toward an Entangling Alliance*, xiv, xvii.
294. Powaski, *Toward an Entangling Alliance*, xx.

become us. The American solipsism is that Americans see the world as a planet totally populated by "frustrated or potential Americans."[295] Such errant egoism is born in the ignorance of isolationism, and it serves as a justification for imposing American solutions and the American way [the only true "self"] on the rest of the world. [296]

ISOLATIONISM IN THE TWENTIETH CENTURY

With the brief exception of the Spanish American War (which was aimed primarily at Asia, not at Europe) and Teddy Roosevelt's subsequent turn-of-the-century manipulations in Central America, US isolationism would remain inviolate until World War I. After that war, again fearing future European entanglements, the United States returned to her isolationist ways, refusing the League of Nations. Taking as its motto "what is good for the United States is good for the world," America initiated "a foreign policy of self indulgence that reflected the hedonistic mood of the 1920s."[297] In the throws of the Great Depression of the 1930s, Americans chose simply to "ignore the world." The sense of mission, which had briefly fueled the nation's rise to world power, had worn itself out in Wilson's great crusade to muster support for American efforts in World War I and in the debates regarding international alliances that followed that conflict. By the time Franklin Roosevelt took office, most Americans were "content to drift."[298] It would take Pearl Harbor to shake the nation free from her womb of security and deliver the gigantic infant of America kicking and screaming into the modern world.

Despite a resurgence of the American isolationist impulse after the Second World War, a return to political and economic seclusion appeared unrealistic. In the years following the war, having no experience in international coalition diplomacy, the United States experienced unfamiliar frustrations and stresses in attempting to shape and execute a cohesive foreign policy. Prejudices and misconceptions, built up over generations of isolationism, made matters worse. As the Soviets embraced all of Eastern Europe, the mood of uncertainty grew. The idea of European inferiority, long embedded in historic isolationism, was difficult for Americans to ignore, especially when it came to the non-Caucasian peoples of Europe. At the same time, America seemed unable to put into perspective her own material and political success. "Americans were all too prone to take the measure of other peoples by her own yardstick," writes Selig Adler in *The Isolationist Impulse*. The nation seemed to take for granted her singular abun-

---

295. Baritz, "God's Country and American Know-How," 475.
296. Baritz, "God's Country and American Know-How," 470.
297. Divine, *Reluctant Belligerent*, 2.
298. Divine, *Reluctant Belligerent*, 12.

dance, which had moderated class conflicts, created strong national community and made every citizen a believer in the free enterprise system. The post-war appearance of sizeable blocks of socialists and communists in France and Italy was thus beyond America's comprehension. Americans spoke a single language and generally had no understanding of or interest in foreign cultures. It was widely believed that foreigners were intellectually suspect, and they were afforded little confidence. Indeed, America's tolerance for her allies was low, especially in light of the fact that she had to rebuild their economies before they could become effective allies. In the American mind, these humble beneficiaries of her august benevolence were singularly ungrateful. [299] Adler summarizes the American post-war viewpoint well, "On this side of the ocean there was a paradise of abundance and domestic security; on the other, there was a hell of poverty, hunger, and anarchy."[300]

Desperately clutching all of her prejudicial and xenophobic baggage, America assumed the role of world leader. She was a young inpatient nation, unprepared for diplomatic nuance and often lacking the experience, skill, and persistence to navigate the shoals of the nuclear age. In her heart, she longed for isolationism, but in her head, she knew that the communists were waiting for her to falter. Meanwhile, the bomb had changed everything. Fueled by her faithful handmaidens, preeminence, uniqueness, mission, and destiny, the flame of American isolationism burned secretly well into the twentieth century. For years after Hiroshima, this resilient inwardly turned American isolationist spark, thought to have been extinguished by that far greater inferno, still glowed, hidden away in the depths of the national soul. In its absence, another celebrated American flame began to grow—the old familiar notion that all the world had to do to find perfection was to follow her shinning example. Could it be that the unfettered freedom of action that comes with our recent unilateralist tendencies is really noting less that isolationism in disguise?

---

299. Adler, *Isolationist Impulse*, 371.
300. Adler, *Isolationist Impulse*, 381.

CHAPTER 8: MANIFEST DESTINY AND CONTINENTAL EXPANSION

The ink was barely dry on the Monroe Doctrine before a brazen lust for continental expansionism seized the American mind. The simultaneous national urge toward isolationism and expansion constituted a puzzling American paradox.American notions of providential chosen-ness and mission that had been simmering since the first Puritan set foot in the New World finally boiled over in the early 1840s when the preposterously egotistical notion of Manifest Destiny was first employed to justify a vast territorial expansion. According to historian Albert Weinberg, "Manifest Destiny, the once honored expansionist slogan, expressed a dogma of supreme self-assurance and ambition — that America's incorporation of all adjacent [and later, not so adjacent] lands was the virtually inevitable fulfillment of a moral mission delegated to the nation by Providence."[301]

The American mind had always harbored an unshakable belief in the superiority and universality of the American ideals of freedom, liberty, and democracy. From the beginning, Americans had been certain that their ideology would lead the world to better things. The increasingly self-righteous cause of spreading such world-saving ideals quite naturally translated into a providential and historically sanctioned right to expansion. Never mind that, in practice, this notion ran contrary to America's stated ideals. As Weinberg put it, "no matter how equal men might be at birth, Americans had become subsequently a superior people."[302] With that, he describes another American paradox. "The very peoples who had drunk most deeply of the new humanitarian nationalism

---

301. Weinberg, *Manifest Destiny*, 1-2.
302. Weinberg, *Manifest Destiny*, 126.

succumbed most readily to the expansionist intoxication that led the nation into the age of imperialism."[303]

Arthur M. Schlesinger Jr. attempted to explain these American paradoxes in "America, Experiment or Destiny," by pointing to a fundamental dualism. According to Schlesinger, the American mind is divided. On one hand there is "tradition," the real-world idealistic enlightened vision of the Founding Fathers for liberal republican experiments. On the other hand, there is American ideological cover, "anti-tradition," which employs mythical other-worldly means and views Americans as "the chosen people."[304] In many spheres anti-tradition has triumphed over tradition, "resulting in the well-known belief of the supremacy of the America over other nations and people."[305]

European observers of nineteenth century American expansionism were quick to note the contradiction between America's professed ideology and her actions. The Russian historian I. Dementyev points to the sources of American optimism, postulating that free access to seemingly limitless land and "more mobile class distinctions" combined to inspire hopeful American democratic institutions. However, Dementyev is quick to add that, at the same time, many Americans "misinterpreted these traditions in nationalistic and expansionist theories" that were "the ferment for the myths about national exclusiveness." In turn, according to Dementyev, the rapid successful incorporation of new territories "generated the long-lasting illusion that many social collisions could be settled through expansion. In the nineteenth century, the American mind clung to the notion that the realization of "almost all religious, political, and social ideals was ...linked to territorial expansion." [306]

THE ROOTS OF MANIFEST DESTINY

The American Doctrine of Manifest Destiny has religious roots. European notions of providentially sanctioned Christian destiny and territorial conquest go back at least as far as the Crusades. At the beginning of the Age of Exploration in the 15th century, Pope Alexander VI vividly illustrated the sheer audacity of Europe's faith in her Christian superiority and destiny. In 1493, he somewhat arbitrarily, drew a line on the globe, effectively dividing the non-Christian world between Spain and Portugal. Although the other Christian nations of Europe would generally ignore this so-called Line of Demarcation, they all recognized a God-given right to any land occupied by non-Christian peoples.[307] Not only

303. Weinberg, *Manifest Destiny*, 11.
304. Schlesinger Jr., "America, Experiment or Destiny?" 507.
305. Gutfeld, *American Exceptionalism*, 31.
306. Dementyev, *Imperialists and Anti-imperialists*, 23.
307. Ergang, *Europe: From the Renaissance to Waterloo*, 102-3.

were the continents of Africa, Asia, and the Americas thus considered "theoretically free to be taken," but the discovery, conquest, and occupation of these territories were viewed by all Christian nations as "sacred undertakings."[308]

The Puritans firmly believed the colonization of America to be a "sacred undertaking." As the "bearers of true Christian mission," they saw their "New Canaan" as a "promised land" to be "re-conquered and reworked for the glory of God and His select forces."[309] From the beginning, it was "manifestly" clear, at least to the Puritans and to subsequent European colonists, that native Americans did not number among God's "select forces." In Puritan New England, Native Americans were quickly brushed aside to make way for the establishment of a growing, Protestant "New Jerusalem."

This required both force and justification. Although the quest to establish a "New Jerusalem" constituted sufficient license for the Puritans, simply calling English expansion into the American hinterland a "sacred undertaking" in the name of the Almighty, lacked legal authority. In 1630, a civil justification for what amounted to the theft of Indian lands came when John Winthrop declared the America wilderness *vacuum domicilum,*" or legally, "waste." According to this doctrine, because the Indians had failed to "subdue" the land by methods recognized by English law, they therefore had no natural right to it.[310]

For the Puritans, the only law was God's law, and so, like everything else, they gave *vacuum domicilum* religious grounding, citing Biblical authority derived from God's command to cultivate the earth. Put simply, the white race used land according to the intension of the Creator, and Indians did not. According to Winthrop, the Indians "enclose no land, neither have any settled habitation, nor any tame cattle to improve the land by, and so, have no natural right to those countries. So, if we leave them sufficient for their use," he concluded, "we may lawfully take the rest, there being more than enough for them and us."[311] Whatever the intension of the Creator, about this last Winthrop was wrong. There was not more than enough land to go around.

Only a people who harbored a fundamentally racist disdain for aboriginal peoples would refuse to see through the thin veneer of the doctrine of *vacuum domicilum.* Even though the Cherokees had made considerable progress toward European-style civilization, not only in farms, but also in schools and churches and even printing, by the early 1830s virtually all the Indian tribes east of the Mississippi had taken their "enforced departure," victims of America's "destiny" to further the cause of "civilization."[312]

---

308. Stephanson, *Manifest Destiny,* 6.
309. Stephanson, *Manifest Destiny,* 6.
310. Jennings, *Invasion of America.*
311. John Winthrop, *History of New England,* 1:349, quoted in Weinberg, *Manifest Destiny,* 75.
312. Weinberg, *Manifest Destiny,* 73.

All of this was accomplished in spite of the United States government's full and formal recognition of the Native Americans' right to their land. In 1786, Thomas Jefferson wrote, "Not a foot of land will ever be taken from the Indians without their consent."[313] Jefferson, too, was wrong. Like Jefferson, many early American leaders had at least paid lip service to lifting up the Indian cultures into the pure light of Western civilization through education and association, but such ideals were not widely held. With the passage of the Indian Removal Bill of 1830 came the total abandonment of Jeffersonian liberal hopes, just as the Cherokee were approaching the realization of such hopes.[314] Indian tribes were promised a new home in the west, but by the 1870s encroachment was renewed despite "perpetual government guarantees."

Although the doctrine had yet to be named, from the very beginning, the removal of Native American populations from their hereditary lands had been justified by moral arguments that were later to be incorporated under the name, Manifest Destiny. Justification for expansion rested upon God's command to till the earth, the perpetuation of the chosen race, and the intrinsic value of spreading American "civilization." Such arrogant ideals were blind to the violence such justifications did to the nation's espoused budding moral instincts. America closed its eyes to the realties voiced by the governor of Georgia, "Treaties with the Indian were expedients by which ignorant, intractable, and savage peoples were induced ... to yield what civilized peoples had the right to possess."[315] Much later, Charles Francis Adams would put it better when he observed, "Divine missions are things the assumptions and fulfillment of which are apt to be at variance."[316]

THE EMANCIPATOR OF MANKIND

By the time the American Revolution began, notions of providential destiny had been widely secularized in the colonies. American "chosen-ness" was no longer viewed as expressly ecclesiastical; it had transcended the boundaries of religion and extend to worldly realms. Many of the founders of the new nation believed that America was destined to lead all the nations of the earth to a new era of liberty, democracy, and freedom. As Thomas Paine put it, America's cause was "the cause of mankind."[317] Benjamin Franklin proudly asserted, "Providence itself has called America to a post of honor in the struggle for dignity and

---

313. Thomas Jefferson, *Writings*, 4:166, quoted in Weinberg, *Manifest Destiny*, 72.
314. Weinberg, *Manifest Destiny*, 88.
315. Stephanson, *Manifest Destiny*, 26.
316. Adams, *Imperialism and the Tracks of Our Forefathers*, 16.
317. Thomas Paine, "Common Sense," in *Writings*, I, 68.

happiness of human nature,"[318] and John Adams spoke of the "illumination and emancipation of mankind."[319]

Originally, such visions were undoubtedly pure. America's light of freedom was destined to extend without restriction to the world at large. When Thomas Jefferson spoke of a the new nation as a "standing monument," he was expressing a devotion to democracy for its own sake. Jefferson envisioned an America that would lead by example.

Soon many Americans began to advocate the active enlargement of Jefferson's "empire of freedom." As the 18th century progressed, American ideology was expressly used as justification for expansionist aspirations. Territorial expansion, justified in colonial times by the providential mission to expand "civilization," now advanced under the equally providential and righteous banner of the "extension of the area of American freedom." The result was an essentially egoist program of extending American territory licensed by the notion that geographical expansion was a step in the liberation of universal man.[320] The problem, as Professor Weinberg notes, was "that the expansionists are more likely to select their missions with less reference to the needs of the beneficiaries than to those of the benefactors."[321] When America annexed Texas, it was not to free Texans. Texas was already a republican nation. It was to secure territory for American pioneers and thus to extend American institutions.[322]

Onto this stage in the late 1830s and early 1840s walked the brash Jacksonian Democrat, John O'Sullivan, a writer for the *Democratic Review* and the man credited with coining the phrase, "Manifest Destiny." Perhaps more forcefully than any before or after, for over a decade O'Sullivan proclaimed the nation's inner sense of superiority and mission. A brief example of O'Sullivan's flowery rhetoric will more than suffice:

> The far-reaching, boundless future will be an era of American greatness. In its magnificent domains of space and time, the nation of many nations is destined to manifest to mankind the excellence of divine principles; to establish on the earth the noblest temple ever dedicated to the worship of the Most High — the Sacred and the True.[323]

In an 1893 article entitled "The Great Nation of Futurity," O'Sullivan declared America a "chosen" nation with the most perfect democracy in the world, and urged that the "democratising mission" should be spread to Texas, Cuba, Oregon, California, Canada, and Mexico. "Its floor shall be the hemisphere," he wrote, "its roof the firmament of the star-studded heavens, and its

---

318. Weinberg, *Manifest Destiny*, 17.
319. John Adams, Notes for "A Dissertation on the Canon and Feudal Law" (1765).
320. Stephanson, *Manifest Destiny*, 22.
321. Weinberg, *Manifest Destiny*, 189.
322. Weinberg, *Manifest Destiny*, 121-2.
323. John O'Sullivan, *Democratic Review* quoted in Stephanson, *Manifest Destiny*, 40.

congregation an Union of Many Republics, comprising hundreds of happy millions...governed by God's natural and moral law of equality."[324] Since Americans thought themselves opposed to social injustice, O'Sullivan's flowery rhetoric had widespread appeal despite its transparently unrealistic optimism and patently egotistical idealism. Indeed, the thinly populated open spaces of California, Texas, and Oregon would be one thing; and the teeming Hispanic and native-American masses of Cuba and Mexico would be quite another.

It is no wonder that Canadians and Mexicans resent it when the United States uses the very name "America" as if it applied only to the part of the continent that we control!

In 1845, O'Sullivan penned the words that were to sum up the nation's expansionist visions when he wrote of "the right of our manifest destiny to overspread and to possess the whole continent which providence has given us for the development of the greatest experiment of liberty and federated self-government."[325] Shortly after O'Sullivan introduced the term "Manifest Destiny" into the language, America went to war with Mexico and eventually added to her dominions all lands north of the Rio Grande and the thirty-second parallel to the Pacific Ocean.

The Mexican War

The history of the Mexican War and the events leading up to that conflict clearly illustrate the ongoing tension between American values and American action. As Glenn Price puts it in *Origins of the Mexican War*, "It provides an extensive documentation of the uncontrolled internal contradiction between professed values and patterns of action."[326] In the 1840s, America wrapped herself in lofty values in order to justify an aggressive war and disguise her lust for the territories of the American Southwest.

According to Price the cold historical record of President James Polk's political, diplomatic, and military schemes aimed at securing the territory then known as Alta California for the United States is as follows:

> ... he had tried to bribe Mexican officials; he had sought to encourage revolutionary forces in that Mexican province; he had used the threat of force to frighten Mexico into selling the territory; and ... he had sought to initiate war by proxy in order to achieve his ends without assuming the responsibility for an aggressive war.[327]

---

324. John O'Sullivan, "The Great Nation of Futurity," quoted in Dementyev, *Imperialist and Anti-Imperialist*, 26.
325. John O'Sullivan, *Morning Star*, December 27, 1845, quoted in Stephanson, *Manifest Destiny*, 42.
326. Price, *Origins of the War with Mexico*, 9.
327. Price, *Origins of the War with Mexico*, 171.

In the end, Polk deliberately provoked the war by marching American troops into Mexican settlements while he positioned other forces to occupy California.

The contrast between this unlovely tale and Polk's rhetoric during this period is chilling. Polk began his term in 1845, assuring the nation that America possessed the "most admirable and wisest system of well-organized self-government among men ever devised by the human mind."[328] Throughout Polk's presidency he assured the nation of God's continued favor and the righteousness of its national mission:

> No country has been so much favored, or should acknowledge with deeper reverence the manifestations of the divine protection. An all-wise creator directed and guarded us in our infant struggle for freedom and has constantly watched over our surprising progress until we have become one of the great nations of the earth.[329]

At the close of his term after the United States had acquired half of Mexico in a trumped up war with that nation, he had the audacity to claim, "It has been our cherished policy to cultivate peace and good will with all nations and this policy has steadily been employed my me."[330] Two days later, he addressed congress:

> The gratitude of the nation to the Sovereign Arbiter of All Human Events should be commensurate with the boundless blessing we enjoy. Peace, plenty, and contentment reign throughout our borders, and out beloved country presents a sublime moral spectacle to the world.[331]

In reality, the spectacle the US would present the rest of the world was something quite different. As early as 1845, Europeans saw the expansionist handwriting on the wall. Referring to American "lust for conquest" the French Prime Minister was alarmed. "The conquest of Mexico would be a wide step towards the enslavement of the world by the United States," he wrote.[332]

Europe may have been alarmed by US aggression, but in a way America was just exhibiting her European pedigree. Beginning in the end of the fifteenth century, European nations had conquered and exploited other peoples all over the world. As Price puts it, "The effective use of organized violence enabled Western Christendom, developing from the medieval feudal structure and

---

328. James Polk, Inaugural Address, March 4, 1845, quoted in Price, *Origins of the War with Mexico*, 9.

329. James Polk, Third Annual Address, December 7, 1847, quoted in Price, *Origins of the War with Mexico*, 10.

330. James Polk, Message, December 7, 1848, quoted in Price, *Origins of the War with Mexico*, 10.

331. James Polk, Message given December 5, 1848, quoted in Price, *Origins of the War with Mexico*, 10.

332. Francois Guizot, *Journal des Debats*, translated into English and published in "California" in *The American Review*, III, January 1846, 82-99, quoted in Price, *Origins of the War with Mexico*, 4.

building a commercial-industrial-political base on the North Atlantic, to achieve dominance over most of the world."[333] Such violence runs contrary to the Christian and humanist ethical systems of the West. Nonetheless the violence of conquest persisted, even in America where those values were thought to have risen to a higher calling, where the nation thought itself unique—a society created to avoid such errors. But the record of American aggression is consistent beginning with the elimination of the native populations, and continuing through the revolution, the campaigns against the Spanish in Florida, and the unsuccessful invasion of Canada in the War of 1812. In the face of all of this, the United State produced a rhetoric of righteousness unmatched in Europe. The history of the Mexican war provides an unlovely and poignant example. In the 1840s the contrast between violence as a means to an expansionist end and the rhetoric of unequaled national virtue is especially vivid owing to the fact that at that time American virtue was largely "undiluted by sobering experience," and "American uniqueness was still untouched by any felt ambiguities."[334]

Indeed, in the late 1840s few American were inclined to contemplate ambiguities. The South stood fixedly behind the institution of slavery, and as the nation expanded Southerners desperately sought to ensure that slave-owning states were admitted to the Union at least in proportion to free states. The annexation of Texas had seemingly balanced the issue, but prospects for the acquisition of California and the great America Southwest sparked new tensions. For many firm abolitionists in the North, the Mexican war was the result of a Southern conspiracy to add more slave-holding territory to the United States. In 1850, the New England clergyman Abiel Abbot Livermore published *The War with Mexico Reviewed*. In it, he strongly condemned those who would wage war under the pretext of spreading America's moral preeminence while at the same time advocating the expansion of slavery:

> War has, in former times, made salves of its captives; but it reserved to this advanced period of the world its chief exploit of seeking to convert the land of freedom, which it had conquered, into the area of slavery, and of spreading over the new parallels of latitude the blight of national injustice and eternal wretchedness.[335]

Whatever the nation's motives may have been, many contemporary historians charge that America has written a shamelessly revisionist history to cover the tracks of her aggression. Such slanted history is surely motivated by an ongoing irreconcilable conflict in the national mind between the nation's pension for violence and aggression and her proclaimed lofty national values. In "The Martial Spirit," Arthur Schlesinger, Jr. states that James Polk "precipitated hostilities by marching troops into a strip of land claimed by both countries, and when the Mexicans resisted he blamed them for starting the war."[336] A year later

---

333. Price, *Origins of the War with Mexico*, 6.
334. Price, *Origins of the War with Mexico*, 9.
335. Livermore, *Mexican War Reviewed*, 32.

responding to a poll of historians rating the "greatness" of American presidents, he justifies Polk's high ranking by reminding us that "By carrying the flag to the Pacific he [Polk] gave America her continental breadth and ensured her future significance in the world."[337] Thus, Schlesinger speaks for the nation in both condemning Polk's underhanded dealings and violent bullying methods while at the same time acknowledging the magnitude of the outcome of his conquest. Certainly, knowing the real story of the acquisition of California, many Americans would condemn the method by which that territory was acquired but few would suggest we give it back.

With her victory over Mexico in 1848, the United States had conquered a nation in which progress had been lagging and republican institutions had failed to take hold. Many expansionists claimed a religious duty to "regenerate the unfortunate people of the enemy country by bringing them into the life-giving shrine of American democracy."[338] Sam Houston wrote that "The Divine Being has been ... carrying out the destiny of the American race, " to civilize the continent.[339]

Despite American idealist proclamations and expansionist justifications regarding the expansion of the area of freedom, and despite her espoused grand mission as the "light of the world," the US sought no political union with Mexico. Although this was partly due to concerns regarding the slavery issue, which were bound to arise in any new territory, at the heart of the matter lay a more fundamental concern. In the American mind, the "degraded Mexican-Spanish were in no state to receive the virtues of the Anglo-Saxon race."[340] The glowing ideals of "the emancipation of mankind" lost much of their luster when confronted with the disturbingly dark skinned Mexican masses. In the end the US bought Arizona and California and "let time take care of the rest." As Anders Stephanson noted, "Nothing was more important than keeping the millions of 'proverbially indolent' Mexicans out of the American political family."[341]

GEOGRAPHICAL PREDESTINATION

Justifications for the new nation's expansionist aspirations also included a geographical element marked by the perceived, God given, natural right of Americans to expand the nation. This notion had been part of the American mind from the very beginning. In 1802, on the eve to the Louisiana Purchase, the *New York*

---

336. Schlesinger, *Paths to the Present*, 192, quoted in Price, *Origins of the War with Mexico*, 80.

337. Schlesinger, *Life*, November 1, 1948, 25, quoted in Price, *Origins of the War with Mexico*, 80.

338. Weinberg, *Manifest Destiny*, 161.

339. Weinberg, *Manifest Destiny*, 178.

340. *Democratic Review* quoted in Stephanson, *Manifest Destiny*, 46.

341. Stephanson, *Manifest Destiny*, 46.

Evening Post declared that New Orleans was within "the limits which appear to be assigned by nature and by reason."[342]

At the heart of this line of thinking there lurked the grand arrogance, which many historians have termed "geographical predestination." This dogma held that "nature or the natural order of things destined natural boundaries for nations in general and the United States, the nation of special destiny, in particular."[343] Almost from the beginning, Americans had seen the Pacific Ocean as the nation's rightful and natural western boundary, even though Spain, and later Mexico, was sovereign in California and the English had laid claim to the Pacific Northwest. As early as 1829, many Americans were audaciously declaring the trickle that was the Rio Grande to be "designed by the hand of Heaven as the boundary between great nations."[344] This obvious hyperbole might have been a joke had it not been so earnestly believed in the United States. As it turned out, it was a double joke for the US would invade Mexico to the south of that stream only 20 years later.

As high-handed and self-serving as all of this may appear, America later employed an even more audacious version of the "doctrine of geographical predestination" to justify even wilder and more arrogant expansionist ambitions. After claiming the ocean to be the most inviolate of "natural" boundaries, America then set her sights on Cuba, later on Hawaii, and lastly and most astoundingly, on the Philippines. Referring to the Philippines, in 1898, one writer would assert, presumably with a straight face, "We are stretching out our hand for what nature meant to be ours."[345] With the carrying of US sovereignty to the Philippines, the doctrine of geographical predestination and the American philosophy of the natural boundary, which had been the cornerstones of American continental expansion, finally "met with logical catastrophe."[346]

AMERICAN CONTINENTAL EXPANSION

The Louisiana Purchase took place in 1803. Florida was purchased from Spain in 1819. Disputes with England were resolved and Washington, Oregon and Upper California became US territory in 1848. Later that same year, New Mexico, Arizona, Lower California, and parts of Nevada and Utah were purchased from Mexico according to the terms of the treaty of Guadalupe Hidalgo.

Dreams of an all-American North American continent seemed to be at an end when the United States withdrew from Mexico, but the story of American

---

342. Weinberg, *Manifest Destiny*, 46.
343. Weinberg, *Manifest Destiny*, 43.
344. *Nashville Republican*, 1829, quoted in Weinberg, *Manifest Destiny*, 58.
345. Charles Denby, "Shall We Keep the Philippines?" *Forum*, XXVI, 1898.
346. Weinberg, *Manifest Destiny*, 70.

continental expansion was not over. Although the nation would briefly appear to lose its zeal for Manifest Destiny during the Reconstruction era, the core beliefs that supported the arrogant expansionist doctrine were still engraved in the American mind. There was speculation that the US would invade Mexico after the Civil War ended, and the end of that war also saw American maneuvering to annex Canada.[347] This ended with the creation of the Dominion of Canada in 1867. In that same year, Secretary of State Seward managed to negotiate to buy Alaska from Russia, but support for this transaction was lukewarm at best and the Alaska Purchase was widely denounced at the time as "Seward's Folly."

The last chapter in the saga of American continental expansion is little read. It recounts continued efforts in the United States to annex Canada. The movement was most active at the beginning of the second decade of the 20th century, and it reached its peak when Congress passed a bill of reciprocity in 1911. It was clear at the time that the United States meant reciprocity to be a first step toward union. Certainly, Americans reasoned, Canada sought to share in America's destiny and would jump at the chance. Certainly, Canadians shared their southern neighbors' audacious view of themselves. Rejection was unthinkable. Thus, the nation was both surprised and offended when the Canadian people voted not to accept the offer.

The rejection was understood everywhere except in the US. Unknown to folks in the States, Canada, like many other Western nations, harbored subtle resentments toward America. While most admired the US, many at the same time reacted negatively to what they perceived to be vulgar American pride and boastfulness.[348] Certainly, in the case of Canada, the US had not approached the matter of reciprocity with humility. Brash over-confidence and assertiveness had undoubtedly made Canadians feel like they were about to be gobbled up by their powerful neighbor. A jilted America lashed out with insults, "If they loved liberty as we do,... they would not stay under the British flag," cried Senator Reed of Missouri.[349] Canada's Sir Wilfrid Laurier heatedly replied, "We are just as proud as you are, and rather than part with our national existence, we would rather part with our lives."[350]

This was stunning. Canadian patriots claimed that they would rather die than join the States. The idea was incomprehensible in the US, where many people have never been able to imagine the patriotism of any other nation as equal to their own. The Canadian rejection went well beyond the understanding of a people raised on the myth that only by becoming like the US could another nation achieve true "civilization, virtue, and happiness."[351] It was another lesson

---

347. Morison, *Oxford History of the American People*, 727.
348. Weinberg, *Manifest Destiny*, 380.
349. Weinberg, *Manifest Destiny*, 378.
350. Weinberg, *Manifest Destiny*, 377.

the United States would never learn. Nor would she learn that the only thing manifest about destiny is that it is not manifest.

---

351. Weinberg, *Manifest Destiny*, 355.

CHAPTER 9: MANIFEST DESTINY AND AMERICAN IMPERIALISM

Although visions of a nation stretching from sea to sea had become real by the middle of the 19th century, even wilder expansionist dreams beckoned, demanding broader interpretations of Manifest Destiny. Northern victory in the American Civil War was widely understood as "divine vindication," revitalizing the nation's sense of mission.[352] As one Philadelphia preacher announced, the United States had been born again, "a mountain of holiness for the dissemination of light and purity to all nations."[353]

Nevertheless, after almost a hundred years in the role of "light unto nations," there was reason to question the founding father's vision of spreading American freedom and democracy by example alone. Most of the nations that had attempted to follow the American example (especially in the New World) had quickly fallen into political disorder. Although disheartening, this reality reinforced American notions of national superiority. Citing "a special understanding of appropriate revolutionary behavior," a unique "grasp of progressive political ideas,"[354] and presumptuously and egoistically disparaging "the capacity of other peoples to govern themselves,"[355] the United States began to presume it her right to judge and instruct other peoples. This gave Manifest Destiny a new meaning. If her shining example would not bring democracy to a corrupt and fallen world, then perhaps a little push was needed. The notion grew that America, as Charles Schultz put it, "could transform any country inhabited by any kind of population, into something like itself simply by

---

352. Stephanson, *Manifest Destiny*, 65.
353. Stephanson, *Manifest Destiny*, 65.
354. Hunt, *Ideology and US Foreign Policy*, 124.
355. Weinberg, *Manifest Destiny*, 122.

extending over it the magic of its institutions."[356] Such transformations were considered inevitable, a faith so ingrained in the American mind that it appeared to be common sense. So, if overt action was needed to hasten destiny, what could be the damage? After all, most Americans firmly believed that in the end American democracy would be enshrined in a worldwide trinity: 'free government, free commerce and free men.'"[357]

Drawing its justification primarily from notions of the superiority of American political institutions, this new vision of Manifest Destiny, with its broader expansionist impulse, gained strength in the last decade of the nineteenth century. For many, faith in the superiority of the American form of government and the American way of life was rooted in the fundamentally racist notion that Anglo-Saxons possessed a singular and exclusive gift when it came to the creation of republican forms of government. In this context, Manifest Destiny was not so much America's legacy, as it was an Anglo Saxon birthright, based on inborn superior political and social ability. The most notable voices of America's late century Anglo-Saxon superiority myth and its accompanying global rights and expansionist obligations were the historians John Fiske and John Williams Burgess.

In a series of lectures, entitled "Manifest Destiny," delivered between 1880 and 1885, Fiske declared, "In assigning our boundaries we must look to the great and glorious future which is prescribed for us by the Manifest Destiny of the Anglo-Saxon race."[358] Fiske's theory of Anglo-Saxon superiority pointed to the ultimate triumph of the principles of federalism and local autonomy among English speaking peoples. According to Fiske, the Saxon's superior "Teutonic" political heritage came to America from England with the Puritans, making America the heir to the Anglo-Saxons' unparalleled natural gift for the development of republican political institutions. Fiske's theories were among the first to combine evolutionism, expansionism, and the Anglo-Saxon superiority myth.[359] He concluded that it was the "right and duty" of the United States to proliferate its "superior" constitutional institutions throughout the world.[360] "Here's to the United States," he toasted in his celebrated lectures, "bound on the north by the North Pole, on the south by the South Pole, on the east by the rising sun, and on the west by the setting sun."[361] In 1885, Fiske published his lectures

---

356. Charles Schultz, "Manifest Destiny," in *Harper's New Monthly Magazine*, LXXXVII (1893), 737.

357. Stephanson, *Manifest Destiny*, 97.

358. Fiske, "Manifest Destiny," in *Harper's New Monthly Magazine*, March, 1885, quoted in Dementyev, *Imperialist and Anti-imperialist*, 43.

359. Dementyev, *Imperialist and Anti-imperialist*, 43.

360. Hofstadter, *Social Darwinism*, 176.

361. Fiske, "Manifest Destiny," in *Harper's New Monthly Magazine*, March, 1885, quoted in Dementyev, *Imperialist and Anti-imperialist*, 43.

in a volume entitled, *American Political Ideas Viewed from the Standpoint of Universal History*. It was an immediate success. In this book, Fiske concluded, "that the time will come ... when it will be possible ... to speak of the United States as stretching from pole to pole.... Indeed, only when such a state of things has begun to be realized, can Civilization ... as sharply demarcated from Barbarism, be said to have fairly begun."[362]

In the last decade of the nineteenth century, John Burgess took Fiske's theories even further. Burgess postulated that not only did Anglo-Saxons possess a unique gift for creating republican political institutions; he also claimed that successful political organization was a function of the ethnic composition of the population. In the *Idea of the American Commonwealth*, he declared Aryan nations to be "political nations," and non-Aryan nations "non-political." "No other peoples have created democratic states," he wrote, "no other peoples or populations have given the slightest evidence of the ability to create democratic states."[363] He followed this with a hierarchy of ethnic political abilities with Anglo-Saxons at the top; Romans and Latinos below; Slavs, Greeks and Celts at a still lower level, and the darker-skinned races at the bottom. Burgess then declared the American Federal system to be the highest achievement of Teutonic political genius, "perfectly adapted for universal application." For Burgess, this system was destined to become "the bearer of the ideal of the world."[364]

Burgess was not content to set American success up as a passive beacon. He advocated active expansionism and urged the use of military force as necessary, declaring armed intervention to be the "right and duty" of all so-called "political nations." He recognized no human rights "at the stage of barbarity" found in "incompetent" "un-political nations." Such nations, he argued, "were incapable of forming civilized states and would therefore remain in a barbarous or half barbarous condition until politically developed nations performed the task for them."[365]

In 1890, many Americans rallied around Fiske and Burgess as men of noble vision, and the perceived nobility of their insight, as well as the apparent inevitability of their predictions, served as justification for expansion beyond the North American continent. Spreading democracy by whatever means was deemed more just than obeying the technical criteria of international law. This is to say that for Americans, the moral issue outweighed the legal issue.[366] In the American mind, the expansionists' motive was pure and altruistic. After all, it

---

362. Fiske, *American Political Ideas*, 151-2.
363. Burgess, "Ideal of the American Commonwealth," in *Political Science Quarterly*, Vol. X, No. 1. September, 1895, 406-7.
364. Burgess, "Ideal of the American Commonwealth," in *Political Science Quarterly*, Vol. X, No. 1. September, 1895, 418.
365. Dementyev, *Imperialist and Anti-imperialist*, 53.
366. Weinberg, *Manifest Destiny*, 145.

was impossible for most Americans to believe that the great republic could have an improper motive. "Without identification with Sir Galahad, it would have been impossible to unsheathe the sword" of imperialism.[367]

A New Departure

As the second half of the 19th century wore on, renewed faith in America's universal mission and unswerving belief in her moral superiority were not the only forces shaping the American mind. Stimulated during the Civil war, American industry was rapidly emerging to take its place in the modern industrial world. New technologies blossomed. Population soared. The vast reaches of the American West were being settled and its abundant resources exploited. The frontier was disappearing.

For Fredrick Jackson Turner, the disappearance of the American frontier in 1890 signaled a crisis for American democracy and the American way of life. It was Turner's thesis that the conditions for the success of American democracy were the free lands and the primitive social relations typical of frontier life. In the past, the development of former frontier areas had civilized wild areas, exploiting resources and destroying the primitive economy so conducive to democratic institutions and American individualism. However, before 1890, the frontier did not die; it simply moved farther westward. In Turner's theory, the frontier was a magical elixir, curing American of economic, political, and social ills, the seminal instrument for the creation of the American way of life. For Turner, its disappearance in 1890 posed a serious threat to the ideals of the nation and presented America with a dilemma: "either radically adjust political institutions to a non-expanding society or find new alternatives for expansion."[368]

Since Turner's thesis explained American democracy and prosperity in the past as the result of the territorial expansion that sustained America's democratic institutions and fathered American individualism, his obvious implied conclusion was that expansion was needed for the future development of the republic. As William A. Williams put it, "Either implicitly or explicitly, depending on the form in which it was presented, the idea pointed to the practical conclusion that expansion was the way to stifle unrest, preserve democracy, and restore prosperity."[369]

As the frontier dwindled, a new kind of individualism and selfish national pride appeared; grasping, self-reliant, reckless, capable. Immediately following the Civil War, aggressive new voices of Manifest Destiny were heard in Con-

367. Weinberg, *Manifest Destiny*, 309.
368. Dementyev, *Imperialist and Anti-imperialist*, 80.
369. Williams, *Tragedy of American Diplomacy*, 24.

gress. When Secretary of State Seward purchased Alaska, Representative Shella-barger candidly observed:

> Our propensities as Saxons, our vanity as Americans, our pride as a great progres-sive nation, our love of dominion, our lust for power, our self-gratification, our notions of what a great thing in diameter our country ought to be, and, above all, our ideas that it is unpatriotic and out of fashion to hold that our future is not to be found in owning all the continents and the islands between, all impels us to take this land.[370]

This may have seemed a little over the top, especially since the Alaska Pur-chase had not been applauded by the majority of Americans. Nonetheless, it was a frank statement of the arrogance of the American expansionist mind, and it echoed across the nation in the Gilded Age. By the last decade of the 19th century, this kind of rhetoric had become even more aggressive. In 1898, a *Wash-ington Post* editorial captured the spirit:

> A new consciousness seems to have come upon us — the consciousness of strength — and with it a new appetite, the yearning to show our strength. It might be com-pared with the effect upon an animal creation of the taste of blood. Ambition, inter-est, land hunger, pride, the mere joy of fighting, whatever may it be, we are animated by a new sensation. We are face to face with a strange destiny. The taste of empire is in the mouth of the people even as the taste of blood is in the jungle.[371]

In this rather dramatic context, American expansion seemed inevitable. It might be opposed by the other nations of the world, but it would not be opposed by the American people, who were "themselves, caught, willing or unwilling, in the toils of an inevitable destiny."[372] The *Chicago Tribune* recognized this enhanced sense of destiny a few years later when it referred to "forces deeper than our formal policies, inherent in the character of the people, inevitable while our vitality remains."[373] Recalling "the old Viking spirit," United States Repre-sentative Gibson declared, "It is the controlling spirit of the people. It is bound to have its way. Manifest Destiny is its platform, its watchword, its faith and its battle cry; and impelled by this spirit and this principle, the people of the United States are even now taking a new departure...."[374]

With this "new departure," America began to eye the world in a different light. Her gaze fell upon the Caribbean, on Cuba and Haiti, and on Hawaii in the

---

370. United States Representative Shellabarger, *Congressional Globe*, 40th Congress, 2nd Session, 377, quoted in Weinberg, *Manifest Destiny*, 232.

371. *Washington Post*, quoted in *Congressional Record*, 55th Congress, 2nd Session, 573, quoted in Weinberg, *Manifest Destiny*, 289.

372. Weinberg, *Manifest Destiny*, 254.

373. *Chicago Tribune* quoted in *Literary Digest*, III, 1916, 552, quoted in Weinberg, *Manifest Destiny*, 278.

374. Weinberg, *Manifest Destiny*, 266.

Pacific. Her thinking was becoming global, strategic. Her navy grew. Control of the world's oceans suddenly seemed essential.[375]

In 1897, Captain Alfred Thayer Mahan published his influential *The Interest of America in Sea Power*. In it, Mahan held that a strong navy constituted the sole determining factor in the destiny of nations. As a spokesman for US expansion, Mahan advocated the construction of naval bases around the world and urged the construction of a canal across the Isthmus of Panama. A subscriber to the theory of Anglo-Saxon superiority, Mahan defended the canal not only on strategic and economic grounds, but also, and most importantly, as a conduit for the spread of American influence, culture, and power. "The fundamental meaning of the canal," he wrote, "will be that it advances by thousands of miles the frontiers of European civilization."[376] Along with the writings of John Fiske and John Burgess, the books of Alfred Mahan pointed with undisguised racism to Anglo Saxon superiorly theories, to social Darwinism, and to and new manifestations of America's destiny, which suddenly seemed to include radically expanded horizons.

The Spanish American War

In 1898, American sympathy for a Cuban insurrection against Spain along with the loss of the American battleship Maine in Havana harbor aroused the simmering new aggressive American spirit. Although an honorable peace might have been achieved, Americans, inflamed by a sensationalist press, wanted blood and demanded war. In April of 1898, buckling under public pressure, President McKinley misleadingly told Congress he had made "every effort to relieve the intolerable condition which is at our door," and Congress rushed to declare war on Spain.[377]

Public support was nearly unanimous for this holy war to "free Cuba." In an orgy of patriotism, "young men rushed to the colors, while bands crashed out the chords of Sousa's 'Stars and Stripes Forever.'"[378] John Hay called it "a splendid little war," and most Americans embraced the effort as "their own little war of liberty and democracy against all that was tyrannical, treacherous, and fetid in the Old World."[379] The use of force was viewed as "a means of fulfilling the destined duty of extending civilization,"[380] an unfortunate means to a necessary end. The unlikely bed-fellows of humanitarianism and force were recon-

---

375. Mahan, *Interest of America in Sea Power*, 21.

376. Mahan, *Interest of America in Sea Power*, 260.

377. Morison, *Oxford History of the American People*, 801.

378. Morison, *Oxford History of the American People*, 802.

379. Morison, *Oxford History of the American People*, 802.

380. Weinberg, *Manifest Destiny*, 274.

ciled in most American minds by the belief that both were components of the national destiny.

After ten weeks of fighting, the United States had stolen an empire from Spain. Despite the fact that the war had been a mismatch from the beginning, victory as confirmed the doctrine of Manifest Destiny and notions of national superiority for most Americans. Following the Spanish surrender, the national press echoed with arrogance and undisguised racism, insisting that victory had confirmed the superiority of the Anglo-Saxons race over the Latin. The *Atlantic Monthly* contrasted the "decadence" of the Latin with the "virility of the Anglo-Saxon."[381] Likewise, the conquest of the Philippines was the occasion for similar journalistic outpourings. In 1898, the sociologist, Franklin Giddings declared the gun fired by Admiral Dewey at Manila Bay to be "the most important historical event since Charles Martel turned back the Moslems,"[382] and in that same month Lyman Abbot wrote paradoxically of the "the imperialism of liberty," in the journal *Outlook*.[383] Along the same lines, *The Forum* published an article by US Senator John R. Proctor, who spoke of US imperialism as "a new Imperialism... destined to carry worldwide the principles of Anglo-Saxon peace and justice, liberty and law."[384] In the same article, Senator Procter hailed the US victory an "advance of the blessings of civilization over the world,"[385] while Henry Cabot Lodge announced "the entrance of the light of Western civilization," in that distant Pacific archipelago.[386] Finally, Whitlaw Reid, the publisher of the *New York Tribune*, editorially pondered the image of the Pacific Ocean as an "America Lake."[387]

When the dust settled and the treaty signed, the US found itself in possession of Cuba, Puerto Rico, and finally after much hesitation the Philippines, over 7000 miles away. McKinley vowed to "educate ... uplift and civilize,"[388] the Filipinos, but they had no desire to be "civilized." This island nation had its own, oriental version of manifest destiny which saw its people as "one of the strongest arms of Providence to direct the destinies of humanity." Filipinos had ideas and

---

381. The *Atlantic Monthly*, June 1898, quoted in Dementyev, *Imperialist and Anti-Imperialist*, 138.

382. Brooks Adams, "The Spanish War and the Equilibrium of the World," in *The Forum*, August 1898, 651.

383. Lyman Abbot, *Outlook*, August, 1898, 1004, quoted in Dementyev, *Imperialist and Anti-Imperialist*, 140.

384. Sen. John R. Proctor, in *The Forum*, September, 1898, 26, quoted in Dementyev, *Imperialist and Anti-Imperialist*, 144.

385. Sen. John R. Proctor, in *The Forum*, September, 1898, 22, quoted in Dementyev, *Imperialist and Anti-Imperialist*, 140.

386. Henry Cabot Lodge, quoted in Greene, *American Imperialism*, 76.

387. Healy, US *Expansionism*, 174.

388. Morison, *Oxford History of the American People*, 805.

ambitions "quite at odds with their would-be benefactors."[389] An armed insurrection raged in the islands for over two years after the war ended.

The question immediately arose as to whether the Constitution would follow the flag. It did not, and this prompted a debate over the legal status of the inhabitants of newly acquired lands. In the end, only partial rights were granted to the peoples of what the US now called its "dependencies." This reeked of imperialism, but Washington refused to admit the existence of empire. Indeed, "imperialism" was considered a dirty word used by those who did not understand that America was "expanding the area of freedom." In truth, America wanted empire, but she also thought that she had "discovered the secret of transforming benevolent despotism into philanthropic democracy."[390] As Professor Weinberg puts it, "The occasion for imperialism arose out of the same war designed to bring people liberty."[391] Whatever her motive for war and whatever she chose to call these territories, America was confident that Manifest Destiny had brought these new lands into he embrace. However, with the outbreak of the Filipino insurrection, William Jennings Bryan wryly remarked, "Destiny is not as manifest as it was two weeks ago."[392]

Throughout the 1890s, the expansionists were not without detractors, and Bryan represented one of the most audible voices of dissent when it came to the occupation of the Philippines. Earlier in the decade, the Populists had opposed expansion in favor of radical remedies at home. The general bent of American intellectuals of the era had been anti-expansionist or "anti-imperialist," as they chose to label themselves. The intellectual protest pointed to the inherent duplicity and contradiction in the expansionist call for the forceful spread of liberty, fearing that in denying self-determination of other nations, American did irreparable damage to her own cherished ideologies freedom. Many held up notions of equality. "There are many humorous things in the world," Mark Twain wrote in 1899, "one of them is the white man's notion that he is less savage than the other savages."[393] However, the appeal to republican traditions and the principle of national sovereignty fell on deaf ears in an era "deluged by chauvinistic and jingoistic propaganda."[394] On the economic front, anti-imperialists insisted that trade did not follow the flag; it followed its own banners of value and usefulness. For his part, William Jennings Bryan had supported America's entrance into the war with Spain, but had later opposed the occupation of the Philippines. In all of this Bryan's motives appear to have been

---

389. Weinberg, *Manifest Destiny*, 291.
390. Williams, "Rise of American World Power," in Bliss and Johnson, *Consensus at the Crossroads*, 59.
391. Weinberg, *Manifest Destiny*, 286.
392. Bryant, et. al., *Republic or Empire: The Philippine Question*, 83.
393. Twain, *Following the Equator*, 192.
394. Dementyev, *Imperialist and Anti-imperialist*, 333.

political, and not heartfelt like so many of the genuine anti-imperialist of the day.

The inevitability and nobility of enlarging the area of freedom and spreading "civilization" to "uncivilized" populations were not the only justification America would offer for her imperialist exploits in the Pacific. Another popular rationale grew out of the old Biblical and utilitarian authorities used to justify seizure of Native American lands: the duty to "redeem waste places." Americans had based their "right" to expel the Indians from their lands on the native population's failure to cultivate and improve these lands as God had commanded. To be sure, the Filipinos were skilled cultivators of the soil, but they failed to utilize their islands' abundant natural resources beyond the agricultural realm. According to expansionist theory, American sovereignty was imposed, in part, out of a perceived duty to ensure that the resources of the world would be unlocked.[395]

In America, this idea had many proponents. In 1898, Benjamin Kidd published his widely read *Control of the Tropics*. In it, Kidd suggested, "Because the colored races will remain at a child-like stage of development, the resources of the Tropics should be administered from the temperate regions."[396] In 1900, Alfred Mahan followed up on this idea in his influential *The Problem of Asia and Its Effect Upon International Policies*. Civilized nations, Mahan insisted, must exercise the "natural right of the world at large to resources that would not be left idle, but utilized for the public good." Congress agreed. Senator Lodge was most vocal on the issue. Lodge openly admitted America's economic motives in the matter, but he insisted that America should "acknowledge no fault requiring apology or subterfuge in advocating for the United States the fullest measure of commercial expansion."[397] For Lodge, as for many Americans, exploitation was a moral duty. Never mind that such exploitation might conflict with an emerging nation's right to self-determination. The desire of a people to govern themselves could not be allowed to "prevent the development of resources necessary to world welfare."[398] Professor Weinberg notes the irony, "It is a curiosity of the history of ideas that the same doctrine originated by the agriculturist to dispossess the huntsman was ultimately used by the industrialist to dispossess the agriculturist. But the jest is entirely on the darker races."[399]

---

395. Wyle, *American World Policies*, 93, quoted in Weinberg, *Manifest Destiny*, 97.
396. Kidd, *Control of the Tropics*, 85-6.
397. Henry Cabot Lodge quoted in Crichfield, *American Supremacy*, II, 640.
398. Weinberg, *Manifest Destiny*, 97-8.
399. Weinberg, *Manifest Destiny*, 93-4.

THE WHITE MAN'S BURDEN

There can be little doubt that throughout her first 125 years, America's notions of Anglo-Saxon superiority were racist to the core, and it is clear that "racism was one of the main components of American expansionism."[400] Subscribers to the doctrine of Manifest Destiny were quite clear on this issue. As the Mexican War raged, the Reverend W. H. Bellows asserted in "The Destiny of the Country," "We have no reason to doubt that this country will not have doubled its three centuries of existence before South America will speak the English tongue and submit to the civilization, laws and religion of the Anglo-Saxon race."[401] Bellows put forward a zealous, evangelical, racially slanted helping of the original American vision of spreading liberty and democracy to a receptive world. However, with the end of the Mexican War, it was decided that the degraded Spanish-Mexicans were, as John O'Sullivan put it, "in no state to receive the virtues of the Anglo-Saxon race."[402]

By the time of the Spanish American War, the rhetoric had become more explicit. In the last decades of the nineteenth century, biological racism had raised its ugly head, as American self-proclaimed "scientists" interpreted archeological findings. W. McGee presented "conclusive" evidence "proving" that blacks and whites could not have the same ancestors; R. B. Bean argued that the brain of the black man was smaller than that of the white; and Nathaniel Shaler conducted experiments that "proved" that the darker races were mentally inferior.[403] Francis Walker published articles asserting that the interbreeding of the races was "polluting the blood" of Anglo-Saxon Americans, leading the their "degradation," and many similar arguments were offered up to stir immigration reform.[404] In 1895, The Reverend Josiah Strong published his enormously popular *Our Country*. In it, he described "God's final and complete solution to the dark problem of heathenism among many inferior peoples." Reverend Strong (speaking for God) pointed out that "the Anglo Saxon is divinely commissioned to be, in a peculiar sense, his brother's keeper" with "an instinct for colonizing." He then predicted that "This race of unequaled energy ... having developed peculiarly aggressive traits calculated to impress its institutions upon mankind, will move down upon Central and South America, out to the islands of the sea and

400. Dementyev, *Imperialist and Anti-imperialist*, 26.

401. Reverend W. H. Bellows "The Destiny of the Country," in *The American Whig Review*, March, 1847, quoted in Stephanson, *Manifest Destiny*, 57.

402. John O'Sullivan quoted *The American Whig Review*, 1847, in Stephanson, *Manifest Destiny*, 46.

403. Dementyev, *Imperialist and Anti-imperialist*, 28.

404. Dementyev, *Imperialist and Anti-imperialist*, 29.

over upon Africa and beyond."[405] The result would be the "extinction of the inferior races" through the force of our "civilization and vitality."[406]

In the late nineteenth century, Darwin's ideas concerning racial extinction were also turned to the service of the Anglo-Saxon superiority myth. Darwin's theory offered another scenario regarding the fate of the inferior races, and for American imperialists seeking absolution, the convenient conclusion was that "lesser races, awed and grateful, could follow the lead of the Anglo-Saxon or drop to the bottom of the heap to meet their fate, ultimate extinction."[407] The 1894 publication of Benjamin Kidd's *Social Evolution* constituted one of the first attempts to apply the principles of social Darwinism to a study of the relation's between nations and races. Kidd's book concluded that the English and the American branches of the Anglo-Saxon race would eventually rule the world.

With the outbreak of the insurrection in the Philippines Senator Albert Beveridge, like many Americans, was skeptical regarding the prospect of Filipino self-rule: "They are not capable of self-governing. How could they be? They are Orients, Malays, instructed by the Spaniards in the latter's worst estate."[408] Beveridge did not hesitate to clearly define the situation in racial terms:

> God has not been preparing the English-speaking and Teutonic peoples for a thousand years for nothing but vain and idle self-contemplation and self-admiration. No! He has made us the master organizers of the world to establish system where chaos reigns. He has given us the spirit of progress to overwhelm the forces of reaction throughout the earth. He has made us adepts in government that we may administer government among the savage and senile peoples. Were it not for such force as this, the world would relapse into barbarism and night. And all of our race has marked the American people as His chosen nation to finally lead in the regeneration of the world.[409]

Here again was the message of mission and chosen-ness, lofty ideals and universal destiny, but this time flagrantly draped in the unlovely cloak of racial superiority.

Such notions of Anglo-Saxon superiority were little more than extensions of the old Aryan myth of a superior peoples migrating up out of central Asia to the forests of Germany, then to England, and finally to America. The notion of Aryan racial superiority had been around for a long while. In the 1850s, American slave owners had coalesced with European reactionaries to put forward the idea of an Aryan master race. In 1855, the French nobleman, Joseph Arthur de Gobineau, published *The Moral and Individual Diversity of Races* in which he pro-

405. Strong, *Our Country*, 159, quoted in May, *Imperial Democracy*, 8.

406. Strong, *Our Country*, quoted in Stephanson, *Manifest Destiny*, 80.

407. Hunt, *Ideology and US Foreign Policy*, 79.

408. Senator Albert Beveridge *Congressional Record*, 56th Congress, 1st Session, 708, quoted in Weinberg, *Manifest Destiny*, 307.

409. Senator Albert Beveridge *Congressional Record*, 56th Congress, 1st Session, 711, quoted in Weinberg, *Manifest Destiny*, 308.

posed that racial distinctions were the root cause of modern social inequalities and concluded that "Aryans" constituted the superior race that was destined to prevail. His work was published in the United States in 1856 with a note from the American publisher stating that Gobineau's conclusions were "incontrovertible."[410] Despite American slavery's violent demise in 1864, the Aryan myth lingered in America for almost a century. Finally, Hitler seized on this same Aryan superiority myth exalting the racially pure "Teutonic" people above all others. Professor Weinberg again is quick to point out the irony, noting that Hitler's embrace of the Aryan myth "made the entire philosophy irritating to Englishmen and Americans who had at first delighted in it."[411] To be sure, America delighted in it in the last decade of the nineteenth century. In 1898, Representative Charles Cochran of Missouri envisioned the "reign of the Arian" pointing to the "onward march of this indomitable race that founded the republic."[412]

Few Americans today are aware that Rudyard Kipling was addressing America's foray in the Philippines when he penned "The White Man's Burden." In 1898, *McClure's* Magazine published the poem on the cover. According to Weinberg, "Kipling implicitly exhorted the United States to take up a dark task among dark peoples."[413] At the same time, the poem carries a veiled caution. Every line drips with venom, warning that dark skinned peoples are "devilish, childish, foolish, slothful, ungrateful and hateful" by nature.[414] They "ain't no kin to me" is Kipling's implied refrain. To Kipling, these faults appeared incurable, but America applied its own upbeat interpretation: "a call to duty — love of a manly ideal — love of humanity."[415] Even the nation's vile myths of racial superiority came transparently wrapped in lacy ideals. For America, racial superiority carried "obligations that could be ignored only at the cost of throwing doubt on that superiority itself."[416]

410. Dementyev, *Imperialist and Anti-imperialist*, 28.
411. Weinberg, *Manifest Destiny*, 309.
412. Representative Charles Cochran, address before the United States House of Representatives, 1898, quoted in Stephenson, *Manifest Destiny*, 89.
413. Weinberg, *Manifest Destiny*, 301.
414. Kipling, *Collected Verse*, 215-6.
415. Weinberg, *Manifest Destiny*, 305.
416. Hunt, *Ideology and US Foreign Policy*, 81.

CHAPTER 10: THE LEADER OF THE FREE WORLD

As the 20th century began, the face of Manifest Destiny had changed. No longer a justification for continental expansion alone, the doctrine itself had been expanded. The American vision of inevitable Aryan westward movement suddenly included new vistas beyond the western Hemisphere. How was America to reconcile this with the Monroe Doctrine? How was she now to avoid dreaded foreign entanglements? Most of the answer, such as it was, came in the form of grand and arrogant rhetoric, ignoring contradiction, proclaiming "a new order of things," and predicting that America was about to take her rightful place as a "world power."[417]

At the heart of this so-called "new order of things," was a burning desire for expanded commerce and enhanced national prominence. On the international stage of the 1890s, a colonial empire was a critical element when it came to displays of national prestige. As T. R. Reid puts it, "By the second half of the nineteenth century, no self-respecting European power felt complete unless it held dominion over plam and pine in some distant corner of the world."[418]

Likewise, fantasies of lucrative Asian trade abounded. Mastering the Pacific appeared to many as a first step toward mastering the world for American commerce.[419] In 1898, Senator Beveridge waxed eloquent on the subject of America's global commercial prospects:

> American factories are making more than the American people can use; American soil more that they can consume. Fate has written our policy for us; the trade of the world must and shall be ours. And we will get it as our mother [England] has told us how. We shall establish trading posts throughout the world as distributing

---

417. Stephanson, *Manifest Destiny*, 93.
418. Reid, *United States of Europe*, 50.
419. Stephanson, *Manifest Destiny*, 94.

points for American products. We shall cover the oceans with our merchant marine. We shall build a navy to the measure of our greatness. Great colonies governing themselves, flying our flag and trading with us will grow about our outposts of trade. Our institutions will follow the flag on the wings of commerce.[420]

Sen. Beveridge was equally enthusiastic regarding future American exploitation of the world's resources:

A hundred wildernesses are to be subdued. Un-penetrated regions must be explored. Un-violated valleys must be tilled. Un-mastered forests must be felled. Un-riven mountains must be torn asunder and their riches of gold and iron and ores of price must be delivered to the world.[421]

As Andres Stephanson points out, Beveridge, like many Americans, saw all of this as the beginning of America's "commercial supremacy," which would make her "the sovereign factor in the peace of the world." "Nations shall not war," Beveridge arrogantly predicted, "without the consent of the American Republic."[422]

Theodore Roosevelt was of a similar mind, although he publicly approached the question of America's place at the table of the world powers with a great deal more caution and prudence than Beveridge and the radical expansionists. Roosevelt never tied of extolling the virtues of the American people. He believed that the superlative nature of the national character had been created when the superior qualities of the Anglo-Saxons race were perfected by the rigors American frontier experience. Although he spoke out against racism, believed that all races could be advanced, and generally avoided references to the "Anglo-Saxon race," preferring the term "English speaking peoples," he was clearly convinced of the racial superiority of this core American ethnic group.

Like many Americans of the period, Roosevelt subscribed to the ideas of social Darwinism, which led him to the conclusion that in order to be a great race America and Americans must be strong. In *The Strenuous Life*, he wrote: "The timid man, the lazy man, the over-civilized man, who has lost the great fighting, masterful virtues ... is incapable of feeling the mighty life that thrills 'strong men with empires on their brains.'"[423] Such a notion, combined with Roosevelt's conviction concerning the superiority of the "American race," led him naturally to the conclusion that the subjugation of "backward" nations by "civilized" nations invariably benefited the subjugated nation.[424] During his presidency, Theodore

---

420. Senator Albert J. Beveridge, *Meaning of the Times and Other Speeches*, 1908, quoted in Stephenson, *Manifest Destiny*, 98-9.

421. Senator Albert J. Beveridge, *Meaning of the Times and Other Speeches*, 1908, quoted in Stephanson, *Manifest Destiny*, 99.

422. Senator Albert J. Beveridge, *Meaning of the Times and Other Speeches*, 1908, quoted in Stephanson, *Manifest Destiny*, 100.

423. Roosevelt, *The Strenuous Life: Essays and Address*, 6-7.

Roosevelt sought to re-define the Monroe Doctrine employing it to justify US intervention in Central and South American affairs.

On December 6, 1904, he addressed Congress on the matter:

> In the Western Hemisphere the adherence of the United States to the Monroe Doctrine may force the United States, however reluctantly, in flagrant cases of ... wrong doing or impotence, to the exercise of an international police power.[425]

It was a day that would bear consequences that went far beyond the imagination of any American at the turn of the century.

Roosevelt, Beveridge and the expansionists had their protractors. American public opinion still favored isolationism. Despite the "new speculations" it aroused, especially in the area of commerce, the Spanish American War "did not change the main structure of national attitudes," which continued to reflect "proud and secure independence."[426] Nonetheless, the isolationist position was every bit as arrogant and presumptuously superior as that of the expansionist. Although it justly pointed to American ineptitude in dealing with her new "dependencies" and suggested that it was generally not a good idea "to kill the people that one was trying to uplift," the real motive for anti-expansionist protest was neither altruistic nor humanitarian. At the core of the isolationist position lay the fear that America would be degraded and culturally diluted by contract with inferiors.[427]

Despite the nation's continued inwardly turned, protectionist mindset, America's leaders were beginning to realize that the United States was well on its way to becoming a world power, and they (especially Teddy Roosevelt and Woodrow Wilson) sought to secure the nation's seat at the table of "great powers." Since the success of her own revolution, America had watched as subsequent waves of revolutions sought to end tyranny in other parts of the world. First in France, followed by a flood of Latin American revolutions in the early 19th century; then in mid-century again in Europe, and finally as the 20th century dawned, in Cuba, China, and Russia. All had failed. All had dissolved into tyranny. From the American vantage point, it was difficult not to feel superior. In America's eyes, "the revolutionary reverses suffered by others confirmed their racial or cultural inferiority and underlined their need for American tutelage." Both Theodore Roosevelt and Woodrow Wilson understood that appeals to American feelings of national superiority would help to "neutralize fears that self-assertion abroad might have disastrous results at home."[428]

However, as the new century dawned, the isolationist mind of the nation remained entrenched, ignoring the blatant contradiction of her new overseas

---

424. Dementyev, *Imperialist and Anti-imperialist*, 106.
425. Theodore Roosevelt, address to Congress, December 6, 1904.
426. Bundy, "Foreign Policy" in Schlesinger Jr. and White, *Paths of American Thought*, 295.
427. Stephanson, *Manifest Destiny*, 102
428. Hunt, *Ideology and US Foreign Policy*, 124.

empire. When Roosevelt intervened to help successfully settle a dispute over German objections to the French presence in North Africa, Congress reluctantly supported his convention, but with an express reservation. They would tolerate no departure from "the tradition of American foreign policy which forbids participation by the United States in the settlement of political questions which are entirely European in their scope."[429] In the American mind, North America had to be kept safe from involvements in the broils and squabbles of Europe. Her empire was not to be a product of the manipulations of world politics. It was a gift from God, "destinarian and messianic"[430] in origin. Even America's participation in World War I was carefully measured.

WORLD WAR I

When World War I began, the American reaction was initially one of disgust. Most Americans saw the war as another atrocity in the seemingly endless struggle between monarchal European rivals. In the United States, both sides were initially viewed as guilty and equally wrong. President Wilson immediately proclaimed American neutrality, admonishing the nation to remain "impartial in thought as well as action."[431] Even Teddy Roosevelt urged neutrality.[432] As Samuel Eliot Morison puts it, "The great heart of the country ... was both neutral and pacifist."[433] For the great nation of immigrants, the European war represented all that they wished to leave behind.

As the carnage continued, the Kaiser declared that his U-boats had the right to prevent contraband from going to the Allies, thus putting American shipping in harm's way. Despite German attacks on American merchant vessels, America remained slow to anger, and Wilson attempted to broker a reasonable "peace without victory" in Europe. The German response was unbending. Still, America refused to be drawn in, and when Wilson asked Congress for the authority to arm American merchant ships for their own protection, Congress refused. Finally on April 2, 1917, Wilson told Congress, "neutrality is no longer feasible when the peace of the world is involved and the freedom of its peoples.... The world must be made safe for democracy." [434]

---

429. Morison, *Oxford History of the American People*, 828.
430. Stephanson, *Manifest Destiny*, 110.
431. Woodrow Wilson, a message to the United States Senate, August 19, 1914, quoted in Morison, *Oxford History of the American People*, 848.
432. Morison, *Oxford History of the American People*, 849.
433. Morison, *Oxford History of the American People*, 849.
434. Woodrow Wilson, address to the Congress of the United States. April 2, 1917, quoted in Morison, *Oxford History of the American People*, 859.

Despite the fact that most Americans still feared foreign entanglement, Congress declared war in April of 1917. Wilson accepted the declaration of war with deep sorrow, and in response to public opinion, he refused to formally ally the nation with any European power, choosing rather to position America as an "associate" of the Allies.

Nonetheless, Wilson knew he had to rally the nation in order to achieve a military victory. To this end, he conducted a shameless propaganda drive designed to muster, if not mandate, public support. At the heart of the campaign were coordinated efforts to monger an intense national hatred of the German nation. The "barbarities" of the "Hun" were put on public display, and Congress passed the Sedition Act strictly forbidding virtually all public opposition to the war. The predictable result was an overflow of extreme nationalist feeling and an unabashed exaggeration of national superiority myths at the expense of the German nation and German culture. German-Americans and other perceived "dissenters" suffered horribly.

America was slow to gear up for war, but the English and French held on heroically. Once significant American forces began to arrive in the field and on the high seas, an Allied victory was achieved.

With the Allied victory, Wilson began to campaign for his League of Nations, which he believed would prevent future wars. However, an arrogant, fearful, isolationist America would have none of it. Americans wanted no part of this grand European alliance no matter how well-meaning, even though the president predicted "with absolute certainty" that if the League of Nations was not created, America would be at war again "within a generation."[435] Nonetheless, the majority of Americans feared entry into the League would rob the nation of freedom of action.[436] Opponents appealed to ingrained notions of American mission and destiny, suggesting that entry into the League would hinder the American quest to "save mankind."[437] For their part, Wilson and his followers resolutely maintained that America's destiny was no longer separate from the rest of the world[438] and that her leadership in the League would still wield "the moral force of right."[439] In the end, the nation would have none of it; over stimulated by propaganda, and a victim of disappointment, America again withdrew.[440]

Many historians have observed that Wilson's strengths and weakness reflected those of the American people.[441] Certainly, his sense of national

435. Woodrow Wilson, in a speech delivered September 1919, quoted in Morison, *Oxford History of the American People*, 882.
436. Adler, *Isolationist Impulse*, 57.
437. Adler, *Isolationist Impulse*, 67.
438. Weinberg, *Manifest Destiny*, 469.
439. Stephanson, *Manifest Destiny*, 118.
440. Adler, *Isolationist Impulse*, 40.

mission and his adherence to principle mirrored the broader American mind, as did his "exaggerated idealism, superiority complex, and ignorance of world affairs resulting from isolation."[442] Thus it is not surprising that Wilson's case for America's world leadership in the League of Nations sounded in many ways like the old Doctrine of Manifest Destiny:

> There can be no question of our ceasing to be a world power. The only question is whether we can refuse the moral leadership that is offered us, whether we shall accept or reject the confidence of the world.... The stage is set, the destiny disclosed. It has come to us by no plan of our conceiving, but by the hand of God who led us in this way. We cannot turn back. We can only go forward, with uplifted eyes and freshened spirit, to follow the vision. It was of this we dreamed at our birth. America shall in truth show the way. The light streams upon the path ahead and nowhere else.[443]

This was not the first, and most certainly not the last, public reference to the notion that world leadership was being forced on America against the national will. In time, it would become one of the central myths of United States foreign policy that America had not chosen her role as the leader of the free world, but rather had acquiesced to serve mankind in response to pressures brought to bear by the flow of history and as a consequence of America's God-given universal destiny.

No matter how compelling Wilson's rhetoric, Americans were not ready for world leadership. In many ways, the campaign of hate that Wilson had waged to muster support for the war effort had reinforced the nation's aloof desire to remain separate, while at the same time, it cemented the idea that Germany deserved no quarter in the terms of the peace. Americans thus returned to another powerful and widely held national fantasy: that of their "happy valley of isolation and innocence."[444]

After the horror of war, America again turned inward. Fearing that her acceptance of the League would mean, "everlasting meddling in every quarrel, great and small, which affects the world,"[445] Senator Lodge advised the nation that she could "be of the greatest service to the world's peace" by simply "becoming even stronger and finer and better."[446] Following America's rejection

---

441. Bundy, "Foreign Policy," in Schlesinger Jr. and White, *Paths of American Thought*, 297.

442. Langer, "Woodrow Wilson," quoted in Bundy, "Foreign Policy," in Schlesinger Jr. and White, *Paths of American Thought*, 297-8.

443. Woodrow Wilson, *Congressional Record*, 66th Congress, 1st Session, 2339, quoted in Weinberg, *Manifest Destiny*, 470.

444. Williams, "Rise of American World Power," in Bliss and Johnson, *Consensus at the Crossroads*, 58.

445. Henry Cabot Lodge Congressional Record, 66th Congress, 1st Session, 3784, quoted in Weinberg, *Manifest Destiny*, 472.

446. Henry Cabot Lodge, *Congressional Record*, 66th Congress, 1st Session, 3784, quoted in Weinberg, *Manifest Destiny*, 472.

of the League of Nations, Calvin Coolidge told the nation, "If we have a destiny," it is to be "more and more American."[447]

The war had ignited an American chauvinistic nationalism, and many politicians were quick to exploit it, calling for a new program of "Americanization."[448] When Franklin Roosevelt took office, many felt sure that he would reset America's place at the table of the great powers, but with the Great Depression raging, Roosevelt correctly sensed that the nation had worn out any internationalist zeal it might have once harbored. The expansionist fury of the 1890s followed by Wilson's crusade to garner support for US involvement in World War I and debate over the treaties that followed had seemingly burned out any remaining American ambitions regarding world leadership. The revived isolationism was hollow and reactionary, a weary apathetic desire to be alone and to "drift"[449] in an isolationist fog of perceived American invulnerability.[450]

Re-focusing all of the hatred she had aimed at Germany during World War I onto a perceived "Red Menace," America entered a period of anti-communist hysteria. This unlovely epic saw a bold resurgence of the Ku Klux Klan and the promotion of "100% Americanism" at the expense of all alleged "radical groups" including "Reds" Jews, Socialists, and aliens of all affiliations.

Despite the fact that ominous developments in Europe and the Pacific gradually shattered the shell of America apathy, the nation clung to her aloof isolationism. As Samuel Eliot Morison puts it, "Had any pollster been looking for one idea on which the vast majority of the American people agreed, when under the New Deal ..., it would have been that if Europe were so wicked or so stupid as to start another war, America would resolutely stay out."[451]

By the mid 1930s, events in Europe were strongly suggesting a rising threat to America's ideology. Although virtually every American agreed it was imperative to avoid war, the question remained, how was the nation to proceed? At the core of this quandary lay an uncertainty, "Could war be avoided no matter what course the nation pursued?"[452] After considerable debate, the nation settled on a policy of neutrality. A series of Neutrality Acts followed imposing arms embargos, foreign loan bans, and travel restrictions, but in a seemingly contradictory move so-called "cash and carry" policy favored trade with England and France. In the end, America's neutrality legislation reflected the nation's con-

---

447. Calvin Coolidge, *Congressional Record*, 69th Congress, 1st Special Session, 5, quoted in Weinberg, *Manifest Destiny*, 481.
448. Adler, *Isolationist Impulse*, 42.
449. Divine, *Reluctant Belligerent*, 12.
450. Adler, *Isolationist Impulse*, 136.
451. Morison, *Oxford History of the American People*, 987-8.
452. Divine, *Reluctant Belligerent*, 15-6.

flicting desires to be both "economically in the world and politically out of it."[453]

By 1940, Roosevelt was clearly on a path to help Great Britain win the war, but the isolationist impulse was still strong in America. When Hitler took Paris, and England teetered on the brink, millions of Americans preached isolationism and pacifism under the banner of "America First." When the Nazis invaded Russia, this cause gained momentum, and the cry was heard in Congress, "let the dictators fight it out among themselves."[454] Then-Senator Harry Truman suggested that we "let them kill as many as possible" on both sides.[455] Perhaps the most visible spokesman of the America First cause was Charles Lindbergh, who as late as 1941 saw the duty of American isolationists to "checkmate the minority of war mongers who did not believe in 'independent American destiny.'"[456]

The national fear of war resulted in a transparently weak and equivocal foreign policy when strength and resolution were required. Instead of attempting to influence the course of international events, the United States chose to hide from them. Disillusioned in the first war, fearful of communism and other perceived alien threats, and resolute in their isolationism, Americans grew doubly cynical of treaties and increasingly wary of European entanglements. Underlying this cynicism lay reinforced notions of American ideological superiority. At the same time, the nation began to harbor "the vague but pervasive attitude" that the United States was not only ideologically superior but "morally superior to the nations of the world and that she could better safeguard her moral superiority if she avoided contamination with Old World secret diplomacy, wars, racial hatreds and decadent cultures."[457]

At the core of such notions lay a strong moralist strain that runs throughout American history and is most clearly discernable in the American view of other countries. As America came of age and republican institutions took hold in Europe, the power of churches in Europe, so often entwined with the aristocracy and with authoritarian governments, began to wane. However, in the US, with its dedication to the separation of church and state, the power of the Protestant Church and its strict moral teachings remained strong. This fueled notions of national moral pre-eminence, especially when viewed against the backdrop of an increasingly secular Europe.[458]

---

453. Divine, *Reluctant Belligerent*, 37.

454. Adler, *Isolationist Impulse*, 312.

455. Harry S. Truman quoted in the pamphlet, "Turning Point toward Peace," New York, 1955, quoted in Adler, *Isolationist Impulse*, 313.

456. Charles Lindbergh, in *The New York Times*, April 24, 1941, quoted in Divine, *Reluctant Belligerent*, 306.

457. Morison and Commager, *Growth of the American Republic*, 2:632.

458. Prestowitz, *Rogue Nation*, 37.

WORLD WAR II: SUPERIORITY CONFIRMED

American isolationism ended on December 7, 1941, and all of America's long-incubating notions of universal mission and manifest destiny spilled out, tumbling headlong onto the stage of international of history. The American cause was the cause of mankind. Franklin Roosevelt addressed the issue two days later:

> And in the dark hours of this day — and through dark days that may be yet to come — we will know that the vast majority of the members of the human race are on our side. Many of them are fighting with us. All of them are praying for us. For, in representing our cause, we represent theirs as well....[459]

The frightful lesson of Pearl Harbor, the resulting super-nationalism that propelled the awesome US war effort, the utter defeat of her enemies in both hemispheres, and the fearful realization of the power of the atomic bomb, all combined to reinforce the superiority myth and compel the United States to actively seek preeminence in an unstable world. Notions of leading by example evaporated. The States would don the mantel of assertive world leadership. The mythical "city on the hill" would no longer appear as "a light unto all nations" but as an armed fortress from which America would set out to "make the world safe for democracy" and sow the seeds that would inevitably blossom into the goodness of the "American way of life" for all the peoples of the world. The myth of American superiority, which had been incubating since the Age of Discovery, was at last fully unleashed in all of its well-meaning power and self-righteous glory.

How could America not feel superior? The waging of World War II had confirmed American superiority like nothing before: not only her ideological, political and social superiority, but also her military, economic and technical superiority, especially in the areas of production, logistics, engineering, and organization. In the American mind, victory had vindicated not only the cause of liberty and democracy over totalitarianism; it had demonstrated to the world the superiority of the entire American system.

How could America ignore the seemingly undeniable facts of her chosenness and the universality of her perceived mission? Europe was in ruin; Japan was on her knees; Britain's empire was waning, and the deprived peoples of Asia and Africa were clamoring for the right to govern themselves. Amidst all of this stood America, robust and growing, unscathed, indeed, strengthened by war.

Perhaps most importantly, it was suddenly clear to everyone that the world had become a very small place indeed. Overnight an isolationist America

---

459. Franklin Roosevelt, War Message to the Nation, December 9th, 1941, quoted in Morison and Commager, *Growth of the American Republic*, 2:664.

had learned that "the oceans were no longer moats around her ramparts."[460] In January of 1945 Franklin Roosevelt made this clear:

> We have learned that we cannot live alone, at peace; that our own well-being is dependent on the well-being of other nations far away. We have learned that we must live as men and not as ostriches, nor as dogs in the manger.

Possession of the bomb alone was a compelling argument for American world stewardship, as Truman's Secretary of State, Henry Stimson, confirmed:

> Our leadership in the war and in the development of this weapon has placed a certain moral responsibility upon us which we cannot shirk without very serious responsibilities for any disaster to civilization which it would further.[461]

To be sure, the imagination needed to create the bomb, not the mention the moral confidence required to use it, clearly attested to the depth of America's robust confidence in her mission and to her moral self-assurance.

For most Americans, this all appeared predestined, a further mandate from Destiny itself. The myth emerged that America had been obliged, against her will, to take up the sword of the "leader of the free world." In their popular history, *The Growth of the American Republic*, the noted historians Samuel Eliot Morison and Henry Steele Commager buttress the myth of America's acquiescence to an un-refusable calling:

> The United States had vaulted from insignificance to dominance, and from isolation to leadership. Not ambitious for power, America had achieved power. Rejecting responsibility, she had been unable to escape it. Inclined to parochialism, she had been thrust into the center of internationalism. Fundamentally peaceable, she had been led by circumstances to become the arsenal of the Western world.[462]

THE COLD WAR

The United States emerged from the war the richest and most powerful of nations, and in response to her newly perceived global calling, she shouldered the responsibility for global relief and reconstruction and for political and military world leadership. The American notion of separateness, exclusivity, and superiority was about to unleash on the world her conviction in a new destiny

---

460. Senator Arthur Vandenberg, Speech, 1946, quoted in Morison, *Oxford History of the American People*, 1002.

461. Stimson, *On Active Service*, 616, quoted in Morison and Commager, *Growth of the American Republic*, 2:818.

462. Morison and Commager, *Growth of the American Republic*, 2:795.

for mankind.[463] Henry Luce would soon declare the beginning of "the American Century."

Only Russia stood in the way. War had reshuffled the map of the world. National agendas had given way to world-embracing ideologies. Conflicts once limited to the parochial interests of individual nations now raged between global systems and philosophies. "World War II, with its terrible destruction of the material, political, and spiritual resources of mankind, created immense vacuums, into which American and Russian power poured almost as if in response to natural forces."[464]

Such an ideological confrontation brought out both America's greatest strength and her greatest weakness. The United States is a nation based on ideology. Unlike most other nations whose national identities rest on traditions, ethnicity and common culture, America's national identity is anchored solely in ideas: liberty, democracy, individualism, capitalism, equality, social mobility, and so forth. As Richard Hofstader observed, "It has been our fate as a nation not to have ideologies, but to be one."[465] Or as Clyde Prestowitz puts it, "America is the only country with an 'ism' attached to its name.[466] Ours is a nation founded on a creed, and one becomes an American by converting to that creed in what Emerson called "a religious experience."[467] Thus, America's greatest strength is her ability to put forward a remarkably strong, unflinchingly united opposition to anything that she perceives as threatening to the national ideology. Any threat to American ideology is quite literally a threat to the bonding fabric of the nation itself. President George W. Bush put it perfectly on September 11, 2001, when he said, "freedom itself has been attacked."[468]

Ironically, the same fact, that the United States is a nation solely based on ideological foundations, also results in her paramount national weakness. American ideologies are specific, based on perceived inalienable, and also inexorable, "natural rights." Thus, certain ideologies are viewed as American: individualism, laissez faire, personal liberty, governmental checks and so on. Conversely, in the American mind certain other ideologies are held to be "un-American." Indeed, Socialism and Communism have always appeared to be the absolute antithesis of American ideals. The very make up of the American national identity itself historically precludes such ideologies. Despite their cherished freedoms of thought, Americans, almost by definition, consider it "un-American"

463. Stillman and Pfaff, "Toward a New Foreign Policy" in Bliss and Johnson, *Consensus at the Crossroads*, 213.

464. Morison and Commagner, *Growth of the American Republic*, 2:796.

465. Hofstadler, "The Erosion of American National Interests," in *Foreign Affairs*, September/October 1997, Vol. 76, No. 5., quoted in Prestowitz, *Rogue Nation*, 35.

466. Prestowitz, *Rogue Nation*, 35.

467. Ralph Waldo Emerson, quoted in Prestowitz, *Rogue Nation*, 35.

468. George W. Bush, Address, September 11, 2001, quoted in Prestowitz, Rogue Nation, 36.

to hold any views contrary to "American" ideology. Thus, the national weakness is an inherent ideological fundamentalism, an unredeemable national closed-mindedness. So it is that America's greatest strength and her greatest weakness both spring form the same source.

Thus as the Cold War unfolded, Americans were unable to perceive any middle ground. Then as now, such inflexible notions protected the national identity and lay at the core of American nationalism. All was black or white. That which lined up with "American" ideology, was good. That which aligned itself with any other ideology was evil and threatened the existence of the nation. Compromise was unthinkable. Nothing short of total victory would be tolerated. Both sides draped themselves in a universal ideology of right. Despite the fact that both American "capitalism" and Soviet "socialism" were quickly mutating to the point where neither term had any clear meaning,[469] mutual demonology ensued. "This act of positioning harped back ... to earlier times of [American] election and pre-ordained mission. Once again the world appeared in stark black and white and American destiny seemed manifest."[470] In order to fight, even in a Cold War, America had to do what she had always done: place herself on the side of absolute goodness and place the enemy on the side of absolute evil. In doing so, she automatically defines a fight to the death. No compromise is possible, and no quarter is asked or given. In a fight against absolute evil "victory must be absolute and surrender unconditional."[471]

With such unity of opinion and unbending mind-set, Americans exaggerated any threat. Historian Albert Weinberg put it beautifully, way back in 1930: "the extremism of the nationalist's ideology arises from the assumption that, since the dangers of international life are not always calculable by reason, defense should err on the side of madness rather than reasonableness."[472] Until Pearl Harbor, American detachment and power had shielded the nation from most international perils. However, Pearl Harbor generated an indelible national fear, and as the Cold War began, America tended to "national unreasonableness" in matters of defense. She began to equate the "barley possible with the probable or certain, ... the remote with the immanent, and the somewhat injurious with the highly injurious or fatal."[473] This atmosphere of paranoia escalated when China "fell" to Communism and when Russia tested an atomic weapon in 1949. In a nuclear age, regardless of her might, the Unites States was as vulnerable as any other nation. "At the moment in history when Americans attained their greatest power, they were confronted with implacable limits on power."[474]

---

469. Schlesinger Jr., "One Against the Many" in Schlesinger Jr. and White, *Paths of American Thought*, 536.
470. Stephanson, *Manifest Destiny*, 122.
471. Prestowitz, *Rogue Nation*, 31.
472. Weinberg, *Manifest Destiny*, 408-9.
473. Weinberg, *Manifest Destiny*, 408.

American fears focused on Soviet expansionism driven by both traditional Russian national interests in Europe and by communist ideology. In the shadow of nuclear menace, a policy of containment emerged, seeking to check Soviet expansion by any means including, if necessary, military intervention. "The policy of containment paved the way for the enormously powerful United States to expand its influence on a global scale and effectively establish hegemony over the world of industrial capitalism."[475]

To garner public support for this actively interventionist policy, President Truman was advised to "scare the hell out of the country."[476] The widespread fear of Soviet expansion made it an easy matter to demonize the Russians and identify their cause with Nazi totalitarianism and expansionism. Truman described the situation in stark black and white. The choice was on one hand "a way of life based on the will of the majority, ... free institutions, representative government, free elections, guarantees of individual liberty, freedom of speech and religion and freedom from political oppression," and on the other hand "terror, oppression, controlled press and elections, and the suppression of personal freedom."[477] Americans came to view the Soviet Union as "a satanic force, dedicated to the overthrow of every sound and proven American principle."[478]

Against this uncompromising backdrop, Truman then articulated the policy that was to justify American intervention for decades. "I believe that it must be the policy of the United States to support free peoples who are resisting attempted subjugation by armed minorities or by outside pressures."[479] Thus, after years of isolation, the United States adopted a "continuing and largely open-ended commitment abroad." Here was a profound change in American thinking and policy that came about quite suddenly and was publicly accepted with little dissent.[480]

The notions of national superiority revealed by American post-war policy are impossible to overlook. Not only did the United States chose to feed, clothe, and rebuild large parts of the world, to occupy parts of Germany, Austria, and Korea, to defend Greece and rearm Turkey, she chose to establish military bases around the globe and to use her martial might wherever democracy or liberty were threatened. All of this was to be accomplished in the name of global regen-

474. Morison and Commager, *Growth of the American Republic*, 2:797.

475. Stephanson, *Manifest Destiny*, 123.

476. Bliss and Johnson, "The Containment Doctrine," in Bliss and Johnson, *Consensus at the Crossroads*, 134.

477. Harry Truman quoted in Bliss and Johnson, "The Agonizing Reappraisal," in Bliss and Johnson, *Consensus at the Crossroads*, 90.

478. Stephanson, *Manifest Destiny*, 124.

479. Harry Truman quoted in Bliss and Johnson, "The Agonizing Reappraisal," in Bliss and Johnson, *Consensus at the Crossroads*, 91.

480. Bliss and Johnson, "The Agonizing Reappraisal" in Bliss and Johnson, *Consensus at the Crossroads*, 89.

eration, and Americans were certain that only the United States could do the job.[481] Although there was much that was good and noble in the results of American relief and in her subsequent interventionist intensions, questions as to when, where, and how the use her Herculean military have haunted the nation ever since.

Although the eventual collapse of the Soviet Union may have cast a new light on many of these questions, at the same time it re-affirmed American convictions of national superiority. In the American mind, the Soviet demise vindicated American policy and unequivocally confirmed the superiority of American institutions. However, the great duality of ideological world-conflict between the West and the Communists had eclipsed any realistic view of the world since Hiroshima. With the Soviet collapse, the real world was slowly revealed as it had always been, fragmented, diverse, ethnocentric, interdependent, and mind bogglingly pluralistic, a colorful and hostile place indeed for any nation used to viewing the world in black and white and regarding itself as superior to all others.

THE MEANS OF VIOLENCE

Most modern nations were conceived in violence, and as Clinton Hayes reminds us, once national independence had been won by force, modern nations concluded that only force could maintain their independence."[482] Modern nation-states often feel compelled to use force: inside to tighten national bonds and to stifle dissent, and outside to address various threats either real or imagined. In moments of crisis, the emotion of patriotism can readily be turned into nationalist fanaticism willing to sacrifice anything for the national cause.

Violence and the modern nation are inseparable. Many scholars actually define nations in terms of violence. Anthony Giddens defines the modern nation-state as "a bounded power container." According to Giddens, "boundedness and the possession of the means of violence" are the key ingredients for nationhood.[483] As Michael Billig puts it, the very existence of modern nations is generally the result of a struggle for "a monopoly of the means of violence." After winning such a struggle, he concludes, the state itself becomes a "means of violence."[484] Likewise, violence for many scholars is the means to power, "and nationalism is inseparable from the desire for power."[485]

---

481. Stephanson, *Manifest Destiny*, 124.
482. Hayes, *Evolution of Modern Nationalism*, 226.
483. Giddens, *Nation State and Violence*, 120.
484. Billig, *Banal Nationalism*, 28.
485. Orwell, *Collect Works*, 265-6.

In the American experience, the use of force has often been justified as a means to extend freedom to (sometimes unappreciative) nations perceived to be threatened by a totalitarian or unenlightened menace. Such justification is generally an extension of themes of chosen-ness and destiny and faith in the universal superiority of American ideology. Our "morally inspired" violent actions involve the unlikely marriage of humanitarianism and killing. To reconcile such a union, either the use of force must be proclaimed a means to humanitarian ends or humanitarianism must be proclaimed as a subterfuge to make selfish, ambitions appear respectable.[486] Since American ideology defines other ideologies as "un-American" and antithetical to our own, far too often we justify our "humanitarian killing" in the name of freedom only to veil its real roots in the questionable motive of self-defense. At the bottom of America's perceived right to the exclusive exercise of "world police power" lie her fears of alien social, economic, and political doctrines. So far these fears have only been allayed by unswerving and unthinking fundamentalist faith in our national moral and ideological superiority and in the universal goodness of the American mission. However, as the new century begins, it is becoming increasingly difficult to imagine America as the leader of the free world, when "zones of gray are everywhere and there is no clear line between the free and the un-free."[487] Today America's presumptuous leadership of the free world is the product of an uncertain vision of world mastery, transparently masquerading as aid to the development of civilization and the establishment of peace, with scorn for every social, political and economic form at variance with our own.[488]

---

486. Weinberg, *Manifest Destiny*, 274.
487. Stephanson, *Manifest Destiny*, 129.
488. Patouillet, *L'imperialisme Americain*, quoted in Weinberg, *Manifest Destiny*, 459.

CHAPTER 11: THE ARROGANCE OF POWER

AMERICAN INTERVENTIONISM

Over the last half century in America, perhaps no issue has been more passionately debated than the question of under what circumstances America should forcibly intervene abroad. The fundamental debate revolves around the question of motive. Is American intervention driven by blind national illusions, unrealistic hopes, and fears that are a product of a unique American national ideological identity, or is it an appropriately measured response to real pressures and threats from outside the nation?

In the decades that followed World War II, America viewed many damaged nations as unable to survive without American help. This led to the mistaken assumption that Americans could "forget the force of tradition and history" and "rearrange" the world according to her own blueprint.[489] At that time, American military superiority appeared absolute, and the United States sought to use her power wherever she perceived a threat to liberty and democracy. As the Cold War escalated and the nuclear threat loomed, this arrogant American folly was moderated. The Korea War ended in a standoff. However, American fears were not moderated, and neither was American's missionary faith in her universal ideology. Throughout the remainder of the 50s and early 60s American interventionism was mostly rhetorical. Interventions in Guatemala, Iran, and Lebanon were guarded.[490]

However, as the 1960s progressed, American fears and ideological hopes for the future slowly began to color the national perception of the present. In her

---

489. Morrison and Commager, *Growth of the American Republic*, 2:796.
490. Stillman and Pfaff, "Toward a New Foreign Policy" in Bliss and Johnson, *Consensus at the Crossroads*, 212.

vain hope to bring about a transformed world future, the United States has lost sight of her original lofty visions. Despite the obvious tragedy of Vietnam, many Americans are still unable to face the fact that America, the nation of revolutionary destiny, fought a counter-revolutionary war against a major part of the population of a small Asia country bent of self-determination. America still clings to the notion that her lofty, benevolent ideological fervor made her immune to wrongdoing. Many still proclaim that it was "for their own good," that we sought to free the Vietnamese from "freedom's counterfeit."[491] Many are still convinced that, while other nations have "interests," America has responsibilities.[492]

Vietnam was not America's only crime. In the words of Carlos Fuentes, "A mixture of ignorance, necessity and blindness has aligned it [the United States] with some of the most undemocratic regimes of the postwar period, from Somoza in Nicaragua to the shah in Iran."[493] Fuentes cites the Hungarian writer George Konrad:

> The United States ... should cease to be obsessed by its lecture-platform self-congratulations as the strongest, the richest, the freest, the noblest, the most unselfish of nations, over-reacting neurotically to every setback and every challenge, seeing intrigue, ingratitude and Communist [terrorist] machinations wherever other people, having interests that do not coincide with those of the United States, insist on pursuing them anyway.[494]

"Why does the United States," wonders Fuentes, "exhibit such a disparity between the way it acts internally (democratic) and the way it acts externally (through deception, intervention, violation of international law, and if need be violent military actions against weaker nations)?"[495]

In response to the perceived ideological threats of the post war era, America's dreams of a democratic world have become increasingly obsessive. Despite the fact that her motives are largely defensive, the United States has always sought to justify its interventions in terms of a higher meaning, declaring its democratic ideology superior to all others. Thus, the US view of reality is radically colored by lofty visions of a world made over in her own image. Her hopes for success, although well meaning, involve dangerous illusions. As Arthur Schlesinger Jr. observes, "The ideological fallacy is to forget that ideology is an abstraction from reality and to regard it as reality itself."[496] The ideologist,

---

491. Stillman and Pfaff, "Toward a New Foreign Policy" in Bliss and Johnson, *Consensus at the Crossroads*, 212.

492. Baritz, "God's Country and American Know-How," 477.

493. Fuentes, Prologue to *Ariel* by Rodó, trans. Paden, 25.

494. Fuentes, Prologue to *Ariel* by Rodó, trans. Paden, 24.

495. Fuentes, Prologue to *Ariel* by Rodó, trans. Paden, 24-5.

496. Schlesinger Jr., "One Against the Many" in Schlesinger Jr. and White, *Paths of American Thought*, 534.

warns Schlesinger, "confuses his models with the vast turbulent and untidy reality which is the stuff of human experience."[497] Having fallen into this trap, America focuses on her unrealistic hopes for a worldwide democratic future while she remains blind to the pluralistic realities of the present. The result is what Stillman and Pfaff chillingly term "benevolent ruthlessness in pursuit of the unattainable."[498]

SUPERIORITY AND AMERICAN RUTHLESSNESS

Is Stillman and Pfaff's charge accurate? Are Americans ruthless in pursuit of purportedly benevolent national goals? Does America employ unnecessarily violent methods in her attempts to carry out her proclaimed universal mission? Even the most survey examination of US history will reveal the most violent of modern nations.

Indeed, the penchant for violence constitutes a national myth. It is rooted first in the Revolution, and many Americans still feel that freedom won by violent means can only be retained by violent means. Later the experience of the American frontier produced the volatile epic characterized by "the interaction of immigrant and open continent."[499] In this regard, Fredrick Jackson Turner notes the importance of the frontier in molding America's violent disposition. "From that day to this," Turner writes, the frontier acted "as a military training school, keeping alive the power of resistance to aggression, and developing the stalwart and rugged qualities of the frontiersman."[500] Thus, it is not surprising that Americans still cling to their guns despite overwhelming evidence that, in the modern world, an armed population is a menace to the common good not a deterrent to tyranny.

American history is a saga of violence unlike any other: vigilante violence, labor violence, racial violence, range wars, family feuds, assassinations, and the violence of civil disobedience, not to mention criminal violence, domestic violence, the near genocide of a native population, and the ultimate violence of America at war. Our popular culture celebrates violence in the most spectacular ways imaginable. Our literature overflows with violence. Vigilante violence in the Old West is still admired by many Americans. Violent American bandit-heroes abound, like Jesse James, Billy the Kid, Bonnie and Clyde. All of this reveals a boiling, angry, "trigger-happy" nation, where violence is regarded as a

---

497. Schlesinger Jr., "One Against the Many" in Schlesinger Jr. and White, *Paths of American Thought*, 535.

498. Stillman and Pfaff, "Toward a New Foreign Policy" in Bliss and Johnson, *Consensus at the Crossroads*, 215.

499. Graham and Gurr, *Violence in America*, 79.

500. Turner, *Frontier in American History*, 15.

viable and effective solution to problems of all sorts. In America, as Alphonso Pinckney puts it, "[violent] behavior has been institutionalized."[501]

Some of this behavior can be explained by the American sense of providential mission, which has given rise to a national vision of "the individual-as-agent for destroying evil."[502] Here we find Nicholas Rinaldi's "Savior Image," the mythical savior-hero who crusades every day on American television. According to Rinaldi, Perry Mason, Napoleon Solo and Matt Dillon, "live in a world that is violent without being tragic." These contemporary heroes are thus shallow caricatures, and they reflect "a broad-based lack of realistic vision in the society that breeds and cultivates them."[503]

Similarly, Richard Maxwell Brown calls violence in America "the handmaiden of American salvation,"[504] and thus, "an unacknowledged value."[505] The salient fact of American violence," Brown writes, "is that, time and again, it has been the instrument not merely of the criminal and disorderly, but of the most upright and honorable." Americans have employed violence in behalf of many causes, even to secure law and order.[506] This notion of violence to prevent violence leads naturally to the idea that one must fight wars in order to end wars.[507]

Beyond the historical record, just beneath the surface, one senses an inner violence in America that is absent in most of the rest of the modern world, something ruthless, cruel, remorseless, unbending. D. H Lawrence noticed it when he wrote, "the essential American soul is hard, isolate, stoic, and a killer."[508] After the assassination of John Kennedy, Arthur M. Schlesinger, Jr. was moved to ask and answer, "What sort of people are we, we Americans? The most frightening people on the planet."[509]

The deeper answer to this question is that Americans are a violent and ruthless sort of people because they possess distorted notions of superiority and uniqueness. The American belief in the nation's providential destiny has led to a natural justification for violence. The twisted Calvinist notion that whole groups of people were either saved or doomed easily led to the belief that "to wage war against those who were damned and stood in the way was ... an act of

---

501. Pinckney, *American Way of Violence*, 155.
502. Furay, *Grass-roots Mind in America*, 51.
503. Nicholas M. Rinaldi quoted in Furay, *Grass-roots Mind in America*, 51.
504. Brown, "Historical Patterns of American Violence," in Graham and Gurr, *Violence in America*, 21.
505. Brown, "Historical Patterns of American Violence," in Graham and Gurr, *Violence in America*, 41.
506. Brown, "Historical Patterns of American Violence," in Graham and Gurr, *Violence in America*, 19.
507. Gutfeld, *American Exceptionalism*, 98.
508. D. H. Lawrence quoted in Rusk, "Defense of American Foreign Policy," in Bliss and Johnson, *Consensus at the Crossroads*, 216.
509. Pinckney, *American Way of Violence*, 13.

the highest service to God."[510] Later the theory of Social Darwinism captured the American mind. With its implications that the less fit would naturally be either subordinated or eliminated, Darwinism provided a ready justification for the violence of a people that presumed themselves superior to all others. American faith in a national predestination, mission, and providential destiny continues to mark the national character.[511]

In a further extension of this Darwinian justification for American violence, Richard Slotkin and James William Gibson suggest that with every victory America came more and more to view her superiority in war as a confirmation of her cultural and moral superiority. Victory over the Indians confirmed American civilization as superior to Indian savagery. Victory over Spain proved American progress superior European decadence. Each victory recharged the culture and justified not only expansion but also future violence. Born of the American frontier, this kind of logic created a mythology of "might makes right" that Slotkin calls "regeneration through violence."[512]

As America grew stronger, the national myths of superiority and uniqueness combined to create and sustain a doubled standard, which has long characterized American morality. Since America was a nation chosen by providence for greatness, she was not to be judged by the same standard that she applied to other nations. As Henry Steele Commager puts it, "this double standard has acted to sublimate violence, to give it a kind of moral quality."[513] "What was imperialism for other nations" Commager writes, "was Manifest Destiny in America.... Other nations waged wars of conquest, but our wars were just."[514] Other nations should forego nuclear weapons, while American maintained huge stockpiles, safe in the belief that the only nation ever to use the atomic bomb would never misuse it. Other nations should submit their conflicts to international tribunals, while America, being both powerful and ultimately moral and just, could take matters into her own hands. America's hypocritical double standard makes a mockery of her sanctimonious pretensions to the moral leadership of the world.[515]

Indeed, a unique penchant for vigilantism and the taking of the law into one's own hands has been an elemental part of the American experience. At the root of this phenomenon is the Lockian notion that Thomas Paine expressed so well when he wrote, "that government is best, which govern least." Americans have always sought to curtail government power. The vigilante tradition in

---

510. Pinckney, *American Way of Violence*, 10.
511. Pinckney, *American Way of Violence*, 11.
512. Gibson, "American Paramilitary Culture", 14; and Slotkin, *Regeneration through Violence*, quoted in Masden, *American Exceptionalism*, 157.
513. Commager, "History of American Violence," in Graham, *Violence*, 20.
514. Commager, "History of American Violence," in Graham, *Violence*, 18.
515. Commager, "History of American Violence," in Graham, *Violence*, 26.

America was an inevitable product of viewing big government as an enemy of freedom, and a natural offshoot of the notion that the majority has the right to impose its will on all dissenters.[516]

Thus, it is that America's interventionist foreign policy often exhibits signs of this dark side of the national personality. This is especially true in light of our national insecurity that breeds both fear and violence. If American intervention abroad is motivated by widespread insecurities arising from the belief that all alien ideologies threaten the American national identity and therefore the fabric of the nation itself, then America will justify the most desperate of tactics. The threatened beast fights with uninhibited abandon, and since the United States seems continually compelled to view her conflicts as struggles of absolute good against absolute evil, the use of excessive violence often appears warranted.

The Arrogance of Power

The failure of American interventionism is a result of what Senator J. William Fulbright has called "The Arrogance of Power." Writing in the Vietnam War era, Senator Fulbright ponders the "fatal impact" of American interventionist policy on other cultures, charging that America has exercised "power without understanding" with "devastating effects in the less advanced areas of the world." Without knowing what we are doing," he charges, "Americans have shattered traditional societies, have disrupted fragile economies, and undermined people's self-confidence by the invidious example of their own power and efficiency."[517] Despite her good intensions and all of the skill and money and resources she has employed in order to establish democratic influence abroad, America has repeatedly destroyed traditional institutions and ways of life. In the resulting void, she leaves political, cultural, and economic chaos, which in most cases has not been replaced by democracy, free institutions, and an American way of life.

Passing over the notion that American interventionist motives arise out of threats to her ideology, and therefore to her national identity, Senator Fulbright points to even more unlovely roots. The Senator charges that the United States blindly indulges in global interventions with "dangerous and unproductive consequences" because "the idea of being responsible to for the whole world" is "flattering to Americans," that the notion of such responsibility "strikes a responsive chord in the American mind."[518] What is more, according to Senator Fulbright, America's "missionary instinct in foreign affairs, in a curious way, reflects a deficiency rather than an excess of national self-confidence." This defi-

---

516. Commager, "History of American Violence," in Graham, *Violence*, 21.
517. Fulbright, "Arrogance of Power" in Bliss and Johnson, *Consensus at the Crossroads*, 251.
518. Fulbright, "Arrogance of Power" in Bliss and Johnson, *Consensus at the Crossroads*, 256-7.

ciency is evidenced by a our need for "constant proof and reassurance, our nagging desire for popularity, and our bitterness and confusion when foreigners fail to appreciate our generosity and good intensions."[519]

An obsessive preoccupation with foreign affairs is a "manifestation of arrogance," Fulbright warns, "as well as a drain on the power that gave rise to it." The greatness of the United States is not a product of strong foreign policy, but of the maintenance and development of the nation's excellent domestic institutions. In light of what has transpired since Vietnam, we would do well to look to the health of these institutions before we insist on forcing them on the rest of the world.

Senator Fulbright's sense of irony is compelling. He concludes that the "Arrogance of American Power" is a "curiosity of human nature" that a national American lack of self-assurance seems to have nurtured America's exaggerated sense of power and mission.

> Those who lack self-assurance are also likely to lack magnanimity. Only a nation at peace with itself, with its transgressions as well as its achievements, is capable of generous understanding of others...."

> When a nation is very powerful but lacking self-confidence, it is likely to behave in ways that are dangerous to itself and to others. Feeling the need to prove what is obvious to everyone else, it begins to confuse great power with unlimited power and great responsibility with total responsibility: it can admit no error; it must win every argument, no matter how trivial. For lack of an appreciation of how truly powerful it is, the nation begins to lose wisdom and perspective, and with them, the strength and understanding that it takes to be magnanimous to smaller weaker nations.

> Gradually but unmistakably America is showing signs of that arrogance of power which has afflicted, weakened, and in some cases destroyed great nations in the past. In so doing, we are not living up to our capacity and promise as a civilized example for the world. The measure of our falling short is the measure of the patriot's duty to dissent.[520]

For Americans today, exercising the "patriot's duty" and achieving national inner peace will involve overcoming our fears, acknowledging our transgressions, and developing a compassionate understanding of American affluence and power in light of the poverty of the majority of the human race. Only through such understanding can the United States develop self-confidence commensurate with her power.

---

519. Fulbright, "Arrogance of Power" in Bliss and Johnson, *Consensus at the Crossroads*, 258.
520. Fulbright, "Arrogance of Power" in Bliss and Johnson, *Consensus at the Cross Roads*, 258-9.

THE ARROGANCE OF UNILATERALISM

Thirty-five years after Senator Fulbright wrote, it seems clear that the United States has made little progress toward the kind of self-confidence that the Senator from Arkansas proscribed. Nonetheless, American power remains, and as Senator Fulbright predicted, the nation continues to "act in ways that are dangerous to itself and to others."

As the twenty-first century begins, the United States seems to have abandoned former efforts to build multinational consensus along with the multilateral treaties that she worked so hard to create and defend in the half-century since the Second World War. The United States is no longer committed to the multilateralism that she labored to create. A new policy has emerged that includes the use of unilateral preemptive military force—military engagement not only carried out without the help of our long-cultivated allies but in the face of their heart-felt and vocal opposition.

One does not have to look very far to find the source of this radical behavior. The American mind has never been comfortable with foreign alliances. The policies of containment that formed the heart of her foreign policy since Truman no longer appear relevant after the fall of the Soviet Union. In the wake of that fall, a great void appeared. In contrast to the black and white world of communism vs. capitalism, the new world seemed splintered, ambiguous, multi-faceted, and impossibly complex. America had always defined her place in the world in a harsh ideological light that produced stark polarities—our good, their evil. "Freedom is pitted against slavery," Eisenhower informed America, "lightness against the dark." After the fall of communism, a world that suddenly presented itself only in subtle shades of gray was troubling indeed. Without the threat of Soviet domination, consensus at home and abroad appeared impossible, and all of our carefully structured alliances appeared impotent against this new world's numbing plurality and the vague, faceless, willow-the wisp enemy of terrorism.

In the face of such a threat, America has labored to redraw a confused, fragmented, ambiguous world in a way she can understand and actively address—that is to say in unambiguous black and white, in the unmistakable duality of us against them. In doing this, she is blinded by the perceived goodness and universality of her own mythology, and her actions are "frequently informed by ignorance, ideology and special interests that have damaging consequences for others."[521] The dominance of the American economy and culture aids the US in this task, and the nation remains guided by mythological exceptionalism and notions that the American way of life will win out in the end—that all nations

---

521. Prestowitz, *Rogue Nation*, 8.

will eventually fall into line owning to the righteousness of America's cause and to the depth of her material success.

In her study of American foreign policy since the end of the Cold War, Siobbán McAvoy-Levy details the run-up to the recent America unilateralism as it was acted out in the Bush and Clinton years following the collapse of the Soviet Union. During this period, the notion of American exceptionalism was employed by both presidents to reinforce notions of America's belief in her moral superiority in order to muster public support for the increased exercise of American power abroad. According to McAvoy-Levy:

> American exceptionalism ... functions in US Foreign policy rhetoric as a tool for building sympathetic public ecologies ... which enable the exercise of American power in a broader sense. It also reflects, legitimizes and perpetuates a notional identity based on a sense of uniqueness and a right to leadership, a belief in the moral superiority and good motives of the United States, a concern for order and stability in the world, a desire to manage international affairs and to universalize "American values."[522]

In numerous 1991-92 campaign speeches, George Bush offered rhetoric typical of the McAvoy-Levy's theme. Bush told voters that "American leadership' and "American ideas" had "literally reshaped the world"; that its was essential that the US remain a "moral beacon for the other countries"; and that America had a "special role as the world's preeminent moral, political, economic, and military power."[523]

While Bush's public diplomacy rhetoric drew most heavily on Wilsonian visions of America as a "redeemer nation," Clinton often appealed to the nation's original Puritan roots, implying a divinely sanctioned national mission through references to a broken "covenant." Americans have "lost sight of their sacred mission and broken faith with the covenant," he warned in May of 1992.[524] Such as reference to God-ordained destiny is called a jeremiad after the Biblical prophet Jeremiah. Clinton found the device useful, for through its application, he could harangue American exceptionalism while at the same criticize the Bush administration for straying from the true path of American mission and destiny.[525]

Appeals to American exceptionalism always fall on receptive ears. As de Tocqueville pointed out, Americans can never get enough of hearing how truly exceptional they are. Such appeals were particularly effective for Bush and Clinton at the end of the Cold War because, all along and secretly in her heart of hearts, from Hiroshima to the fall of the Berlin Wall, America had been yearning

---

522. McAvoy-Levy, *American Exceptionalism and US Foreign Policy*, 143.
523. George Bush, in various campaign speeches delivered in November and December 1991, quoted in McAvoy-Levy, *American Exceptionalism and US Foreign Policy*, 147.
524. Bill Clinton, in remarks before the Democratic Leadership Council, May 2, 1992, quoted in McAvoy-Levy, *American Exceptionalism and US Foreign Policy*, 152.
525. McAvoy-Levy, *American Exceptionalism and US Foreign Policy*, 152.

for autonomy; if not for isolationism, then at least for the freedom of action found first in interventionism and later in unilateralism—the freedom to re-shape the world in her own image. Despite the obvious interdependence of the nations of the modern world, despite weapons of mass destruction, despite globalism, despite the multinational interlocking threat of terrorism, despite our commitments to NATO and all the rest, many Americans still think it best to go it alone.

At the bottom of it all, America understands unilateralism as an extension of her precious individualism, while she views multilateralism as a form of collectivism.[526] For unilateralists in the United States, European insistence on a multilateral approach to the world's problems appears to be an attempt to tie America's hands. While for Europeans, "the European attachment to a multilateral approach ... is a matter of conviction, not a malign strategy."[527] Here is a distinct ideological divide. As Francis Fukuyama puts it, "Whether in regard to warfare, crime, regulation, education or foreign policy, there are constant differences separating America from everyone else. It is consistently more anti-statist, individualistic, laissez-faire and egalitarian than other democracies." Fukuyama goes on to observe, "Europeans ... tend to believe that democratic legitimacy flows from the will of an international community much larger than any individual nation-state."[528] However, for the US "multilateralism is by definition an infringement on individual prerogative...."[529] The American unilateralist impulse has always been strong. Unilateralism lay at the heart of both isolationism and American expansionism on the nineteenth century. Could it be that the American rejection of the League of Nations after World War I revealed not so much the nation's isolationist urge, but her desires for the freedom of unilateral and independent action?

At the beginning of the Cold War, America followed a policy of containment, paying lip service to her alliances but remaining quick to remind the world that her mighty armies stood ready to directly and unilaterally intervene anywhere she felt her self-defined "national interests" threatened. To backup this threat she ringed the globe with bases from which to project her military might. This contradictory, active, internationalist foundation for American foreign policy involved both conflict and cooperation, and it was presented both to the world and to the American people wearing the garments of anticommunism. Widespread support for this policy lasted until the Vietnam years when dissenting voices began to be heard. There followed a divisive national debate involving "not only questions on whether the United States ought to be

---

526. Degutis, "American Threat."
527. Javier Solana, "Europe and America: Partners of Choice," speech to the annual dinner of the Foreign Policy Association, New York, May 7, 2003, quoted in Degutis, "American Threat."
528. Fukuyama, "The West May be Cracking," *New Perspectives Quarterly*, vol. 21, no. 3, Summer 2004, quoted in Degutis, "American Threat."
529. Degutis, "American Threat."

involved in world affairs, but also on how it should be involved." This national dialogue lasted for twenty years, then suddenly the Soviet Union disappeared.[530]

The American unilateralist tendency has grown steadily since the fall of communism. It has recently produced some rather disturbing results. The United States has recently moved to reject or weaken several landmark international treaties including bans on the use of landmines, bans on the small arms trade, the comprehensive nuclear test ban treaty, the anti-basaltic missile treaty, the chemical warfare treaty and others.[531] Part of the rationale behind these rejections is the American strategy to "prevent the re-emergence of a new rival," which began in 1992. To accomplish this, the United States sought to restore preemptive force as an option and to maintain a substantial nuclear arsenal while encouraging others to reduce or abandon theirs. At the heart of this strategy was the supreme national egoism that Colin Powell described when he called for the maintenance of "sufficient power" to "deter any challenger from ever dreaming of challenging us on the world stage." "I want to be the bully on the block," said Powell. [532]

The size of the military that America maintains to back up her "bully on the block" policy of intimidation is truly staggering. Today America has thirteen aircraft carrier groups at a time when no other county in the world has even one. She can deliver ballistic missiles worldwide from an arsenal of strategic submarines and dispatch laser guided smart bombs, ground hugging cruise missiles, pilot-less drones and lethal gun ships from over 700 US bases around the globe. Even before her invasion of Iraq, the United States accounted for 40% of the annual worldwide military spending, more than the next nine countries combined.[533] Only America has the resources to fabricate and maintain such a strategy, and only America has the unmitigated arrogance to believe in it. Such a strategy assumes the all-encompassing righteousness of the American mission, and proposes immunity from the laws and agreements that bind other nations in order to facilitate her holy quest to set the world right.

In addition to undermining international arms limitations and treaties calling for bans on landmines, anti-basaltic missiles, chemicals warfare, small arms trade and the nuclear testing, the US rejected the 2001 Kyoto Treaty to control global warming, and refused NATO's efforts to present a unified front against terrorism. When France, Belgium, Great Britain and other NATO nations "not only offered but begged" to be allowed to send troops to Afghanistan, the Pentagon took a few British forces and rejected the others' show of solidarity.[534] Finally, of course there is Iraq.

---

530. Wittkopf, *Faces of Internationalism*, 9.

531. Prestowitz, *Rogue Nation*, 144.

532. Prestowitz, *Rogue Nation*, 23-4.

533. Prestowitz, *Rogue Nation*, 26.

534. Prestowitz, *Rogue Nation*, 7.

All of this has precipitated rising criticism and fear in Europe, Asia and Latin America. Despite the considerable good will the US has amassed among the nations of the world over the past half century, as the new century begins, mistrust and outright dislike for America are on the rise. In 1999 and again in 2002, the Pew Research Center for The People and The Press conducted a massive survey of 38,000 people in 44 countries. This survey found that favorable opinions of the United States have recently declined almost everywhere.[535] The issues America considers the most pressing do not line up with the priorities of even our closest allies in Europe, who consider religious and ethnic hatred the most pressing of current concerns. Pollution and the environment rank high almost everywhere but not in the US. In Asia, AIDS and the control of infectious diseases is a paramount concern, not so in the US. In all of this, the United States with her fixation on global hegemony appears increasingly at odds with the rest of the world. Seemingly blind to her frightening rogue behavior, America continues to labor to create the polarized "us against them" vision that only extreme exceptionalism can comprehend—the black and white view of the world that is essential to the maintenance of her cherished notions of national superiority.

Only in the highly charged atmosphere of good against evil precipitated by the September 11 attacks could George Bush proclaim, "we must confront the worst threats before they emerge. In the world we have entered, the only path to safety is the path of action." Here is a clear admission of a radical policy shift—clear acknowledgement that containment no longer works. "We will not hesitate to act alone," the president vowed, in the voice of the new American unilateralism.[536] Only in the light of pure self-righteousness, only in the supreme confidence that everyone will welcome "the American Way," could America devise a strategy of preemption vowing to (forcefully if necessary) "extend the rights of freedom across the globe."[537]

In a world where even desperate individuals can fight back as suicide bombers and hijackers, there is no such thing as absolute military superiority; and even if there were, it could never impose uniformity on a culturally diverse world. The irony is this: American unilateralism seems to be "eroding the hegemony its apostles are trying to enlarge."[538] As the former US Ambassador to Saudi Arabia quipped, "We need a war on arrogance and a war on terrorism."[539]

---

535. The Pew Research Center for The People and The Press, quoted in Prestowitz, *Rogue Nation*, 44-5.

536. George W. Bush, in a speech given at the United States Military Academy at West Point, September 20, 2002.

537. National Security Document, September 2002.

538. Prestowitz, *Rogue Nation*, 268.

539. Chas Freeman in an interview with Clyde Prestowitz quoted in Prestowitz, *Rogue Nation*, 49.

PART THREE: THE PRESUMPTION OF NATIONAL SUPERIORITY

CHAPTER 12: THE MYTH OF AMERICAN SUPERIORITY

For most Americans today, belief in national superiority is not the result of any rational process. Unquestioning faith in the superiority of the nation is nothing less than an American birthright. Such a faith evolved slowly, finding its tenants in the uniqueness of the American experience. Over time, it became taken for granted and embedded into the national common sense.

The early European experience in the New World established in America a belief that, in leaving Europe and its rigid traditions far behind, the colonists were free "from the laws of decadence or the laws of history." As Daniel Bell puts it, colonial America saw itself as, "an exempt nation."[540] Inherent in this notion was the idea that America was separated from Europe at birth, if not before, a nation "born modern without a deeply entrenched traditional socioeconomic and political structure, a nation that did not, therefore, have to undergo the wrenching transition to modernity."[541]

Although it had roots in the colonial experience, the notion of America as an exemplary nation was not fully manifest until the time of the American Revolution. "Only with the Revolution did contemporary observers begin to tout America as a social and political model for the rest of the world and thereby, always implicitly and sometimes explicitly, to claim its superiority over the Old World."[542]

The Revolution and the events that immediately followed gave rise to "a major reassessment of the character and promise of America as represented by the rising American republic."[543] When the Revolution began, Americans

---

540. Bell, "The Hegelian Secret," 51.
541. Greene, *Intellectual Construction of America*, 201.
542. Greene, *Intellectual Construction of America*, 207.
543. Greene, *Intellectual Construction of America*, 162.

looked at the rest of the world and saw that their situation was unique. As the Revered Samuel Williams of Massachusetts observed in 1775, America was almost the only country in the world that did not live in "total subjugation to their rulers." Williams saw America moving toward the realization "of greater perfection and happiness than mankind has yet seen."[544] In 1774, *Royal American Magazine* speculated that in America "the streams of wealth, the beams of science, the stars of wisdom, the light of virtue, and the sun of liberty," would "all unite their rays, and form the sublime circle of human splendor and felicity." As if this were not enough, the magazine's editor went on to declare America "the glory and astonishment of the whole earth."[545]

The rhetoric of the first decades of America's life as a nation abounds with such flowery exaggeration. To be sure, much of this is simply the heady, public celebration of the perceived realization of the new nation's lofty ideals. However, it is also the beginning of the American myth of superiority, for this rhetoric is consistently characterized by the denigration of the rest of the world, and especially Europe, presented in dramatic contrast to the veneration of American perfection. Authors noted "the galling yoke of oppression" that "debased human nature" in the rest of the world,[546] and referred to Europe as "a furnace of affliction and a goal of oppression."[547] On the other hand, America gloried in "the honor, the dignity, and happiness connected with the character of the free citizen,"[548] and enjoyed a "radiant summer" in which men "expected to be made perfect."[549] According to a 1784 account, the United States was "the garden of philanthropy, the theatre of virtue, the temple of science ... [and] the seat of elysium."[550] In such youthful, naive rhetoric lies the beginning of the American Superiority Myth, a myth that defined the new nation's superiority in her emerging ideology. In the beginning, the myth simply insisted that this ideology was superior to any other. Over time the myth became that, by the force of its

---

544. Williams, *A Discourse on the Love of Our Country*, 21, 24, 22, 16, quoted in Greene, *Intellectual Construction of America*, 164.

545. *Royal American Magazine*, 1, 1774, 10, quoted in Greene, *Intellectual Construction of America*, 164.

546. Ramsey, *An Oration in Commemoration of American Independence* (1794), quoted in Greene, *Intellectual Construction of America*, 171.

547. Rhees, *Good Samaritan*, 12-3, quoted in Greene, *Intellectual Construction of America*, 172.

548. James Tilton, oration given July 5, 1790, quoted in Greene, *Intellectual Construction of America*, 169.

549. "The Former, Present, and Future Prospects of America," in *Columbia Magazine*, October, 1786, 83, quoted in Greene, *Intellectual Construction of America*, 171.

550. "Observations in Response to a 'Enquiry Whether the Discovery of America Has Been Useful or Hurtful to Mankind,'" in *Boston Magazine*, May 1784, republished in *Columbian Magazine*, June 1788, 308, quoted in Greene, *Intellectual Construction of America*, 197.

very perfection, success, and universal appeal, America's ideology was destined to become the ideology of the entire world.

Such notions were not unique to American thought. Many European liberals of the American revolutionary era pointed to the possibility of American superiority. In 1777 the Englishman Richard Price suggested that American would "soon become superior" to its "parent state."[551] Writing in 1783, his countryman Thomas Pownall, like few others in eighteenth century Europe, put his finger on the pulse of America by pointing to the understandable sources of future American egoism. America, he wrote, was a place where people could apply their "active powers of industry and ingenuity" to provide a basis for "encreasing population, opulence, and strength."[552] Pownall concluded his praise of America by asserting that America had been marked by God as "a chosen people"[553] and declared the new nation a "civilizing activity beyond what Europe could ever know."[554] As Price put it, "Perhaps there has never existed a people ... to whom a station of more importance in the plan of Providence," had been assigned.[555]

These and many other flattering European evaluations of the American experiment served to reinforce the already self-superior notions that were beginning to inhabit and shape the infant American mind. As Jack Greene put it, in *The Intellectual Construction of America*:

> Throughout the first three centuries of European interactions in America, a sense of exceptionalism had remained the principle component in the identification of America, particularly as it was represented first, after 1606, by the English colonies in North America and then, after 1776, by the republican United States. By 1800, those conceptions ... were deeply etched into the understandings of... Americans.[556]

Despite the growing concept of America as a guiding light, the smug conceit of the fully developed American superiority myth did begin to emerge until the second half of the nineteenth century, and it did not reach maturity until the end of the Second World War.[557] Today there are many myths of American superiority, and most Americans devoutly believe their nation to be

---

551. Price, *Observations on the Nature of Civil Liberty*, 82, quoted in Greene, *Intellectual Construction of American*, 160.

552. Pownall, *Memorial to the Sovereigns of Europe*, 105, quoted in Greene, *Intellectual Construction of America*, 159.

553. Pownall, *Memorial to the Sovereigns of America*, 69, 137-8, quoted in Greene, *Intellectual Construction of America*, 160.

554. Pownall, *Memorial to the Sovereigns of America*, 72-3, quoted in Greene, *Intellectual Construction of America*, 160.

555. Price, *Observations on the Importance of the American Revolution*, 184 quoted in Greene, *Intellectual Construction of America*, 160.

556. Greene, *Intellectual Construction of America*, 199.

557. Greene, *Intellectual Construction of America*, 208.

superior to all others in countless ways. They are convinced of the superiority of America's national culture, ideology, and values. They are certain that American political, social, and economic institutions are superior to all other systems, and that the sum of it all, "the American way of life" will inevitably constitute the final destiny of mankind.

Belief in the universality and benevolence of the national ideology and its supporting institutions quite literally defines America and is the center post of the American national identity. From early childhood, Americans are immersed in notions of national superiority until the idea of a superior nation fades into the realm of common sense and the propaganda and self-deception required to propagate the idea become invisible. America's superiority thus becomes a given, an axiom, a fundamental universal principle, indelibly written on the American consciousness in the language of Divine Providence, aloof isolationism, frontier individualism, Manifest Destiny, historically ingrained xenophobia, and unswerving ideological fundamentalism.

Although no proofs are needed, historical proofs of America's political, social, economic, technological, and military successes abound. The charge of national arrogance might seem reproachful, but the truth of the matter is that it is difficult, if not impossible, to be a so-called "real American," and not feel superior to other nationalities. Americans have been predisposed to their superior airs like no other people in history. If this nation ever had a destiny, it was to perpetuate the myth of national superiority.

EXAGGERATIONS, OVERESTIMATIONS, AND OBSESSIONS

At the very heart of the nation's egoism lies the success of democracy. As Thomas Goebel puts it:

> Confronted with political and social turmoil in Europe, Americans of all political persuasions pointed to the remarkable stability of their country as proof of their accomplishment in Constitution-making. Drawing on the best of what political theory had to offer, the Founding Fathers had fashioned a system of government that managed to combine popular sovereignty with individual liberty.[558]

Certainly the failure of revolutions and republican constitutions in so many other nations beginning in France, continuing in South America, in central Europe, in Mexico, in China, in Russia and right up to the present day, has served to confirm America's pretensions with regard to her superiority in Constitution-making. However, Americans were not content to leave it at that. The success of democracy had to be fashioned into a categorical national superlative. As Goebel observes, Americans have taken their great accomplishment in this

---

558. Goebel, "Government of Laws," in Krakau, *American Nation*, 123.

area and manipulated it into the belief that it represents "the most perfect form of government ever devised by man."[559]

In addition to their reverence for powerful national myths of collective and several superiority, Americans believe themselves to be superior people individually. Notable in this regard are familiar myths of "Yankee ingenuity" and "know-how." These put forward the notion that Americans are not only more inventive, resourceful, innovative and technically skilled than other peoples, but also possess superior qualities when it comes to business, science, and entrepreneurship. These myths operate in tandem with the myth of the preeminence of the American work ethic, along side of which other national peoples are characterized as ignorant, lazy and even shiftless. In addition, national myths of superior athleticism and physical strength have taken hold; the English language is understood by most Americans to be larger, more expressive and more subtley variable than other modern languages; the American landscape more vast, more varied, more beautiful. This list goes on.

George Orwell mocked the great American pageant of perceived national superiority back in the 1940s when he observed a nationalist "will claim superiority for it [his country] not only in military power and political virtue, but in art, literature, sport, the structure of language, the physical beauty of the inhabitants, and perhaps even the climate, scenery and cooking."[560] Orwell singled out America as a particularly vivid example, and although he intended some fun in this, or at least sought to point out the absurdity, like all good jokes, he rooted his observations in a remarkable truth.

Still, what is remarkable about the American myth of national superiority is neither its all-inclusive scope nor its blind audacity. As Orwell points out, such myths are typical of modern nationalism everywhere. What is extraordinary about the American conviction of national superiority is the fanatical fervor with which it is believed and the ferocious tenacity with which it is defended. Self-serving ideas of American superiority generate pseudo-religious feelings, notions of serving something larger than the self, and unshakable certainties that such ideas are right.[561] Many today place "an excessive, exaggerated and exclusive emphasis" on the superiority of the nation at the expense of other critical values.[562] This vain obsession results in an overestimation of the nation and of co-nationals to the detraction of all other nations and national peoples. As Kecmanovic observes, the logical result of such an overestimation is "dislike and hostility" toward other nations and other nationals and "a belief that they are

559. Goebel, "Government of Laws," in Krakau, *American Nation,* 123.
560. Orwell, "Notes on Nationalism" in *Collected Essays,* 271.
561. Orwell, "Notes on Nationalism" in *Collected Essays,* 267.
562. Kecmanovic, *Psychology of Ethnonationalism,* 24.

inferior and deserving of contempt."[563] This in turn results in placing national issues above broad humanitarian issues.

American contempt for other nations has followed hand-in-hand with notions of American superiority and faith in a national providential destiny. Despite its universal intent, the rhetoric of America's presumed predestined mission abounds with aggressive language, threats, and culturally denigrating slurs. John O'Sullivan, the "author" of Manifest Destiny, lashed out at a world of inferior nations:

> For this blessed mission to the nations of the world, which are shut from the light-giving light of truth, has America been chosen; and her high example shall smite unto death the tyranny of kings, hierarchs and oligarchs, and carry the glad tidings of peace and good will where myriads now endure an existence scarcely more enviable than that of the beasts of the field.[564]

Linking other nationals to "the beasts of the field" exemplifies a kind of dehumanization that is often the natural conclusion of American contempt for non-Americans. According to Kecmanovic, this kind of dehumanization is widely employed in the denigration of rival national groups.[565] Underlying the de-humanization of non-Americans is the notion that Americans are a "pseudo-species" created with "supernatural intent" and possessors of not only a "distinct sense of identity," but the only "true human identity."[566] The logical result of such a belief is to place the nation of "true humanity" above all other "sub-human" nations, thus in effect placing the national cause above the cause of mankind as a whole. This reordering of priorities has a tendency to "falsify, to misrepresent the real relations between national groups and the intensions of the people."[567] We are human. They are not. It is the nationalist's classical justification for murder.

Clinton Hayes, who is perhaps the preeminent historian of modern nationalism, is damningly critical of American nationalism. America, he charges suffers from extreme integral nationalism, "a sacred egoism" which results in a "policy of national selfishness and aggrandizement." For Hayes this policy is propelled by relentless use of the nation's power: "inside, tightened bonds," outside, "efforts to make the nation feared and 'respected' ... by bold and firm conduct of foreign affairs, backed by military force and accomplished by 'prestige.'" According to Hayes, this kind of nationalism appeals to "the cruder and more excessively emotional forms of patriotism." Love of country becomes hatred of the alien; national service becomes blind obedience to authority. Freedom of speech and thought are stifled if they interfere with the national agenda. With specific reference to

---

563. Kecmanovic, *Psychology of Ethnonationalism*, 25.
564. John O'Sullivan, quoted in Stephanson, *Manifest Destiny*, 40.
565. Kecmanovic, *Psychology of Ethnonationalism*, 41.
566. E. H. Erikson quoted in Kecmanovic, *Psychology of Ethnonationalism*, 41.
567. Kecmanovic, *Psychology of Ethonationalism*, 17.

America, Hayes concludes, "We have a good deal of cant and even more unpardonable self-deception. Integral nationalism is far advanced among us. We are particularly intolerant of any descent, of all foreigners and minorities in our midst. We are particularly gullible, particularly arrogant, particularly emotional."[568]

UNIQUENESS

Themes of uniqueness have characterized the American experience from the very beginning, and Americans cling to the conviction that in many ways they are markedly different from the other peoples of the earth.

In *American Exceptionalism*, Seymour Lipset delves deeply into those things that set America apart from the rest of the world and concludes that American uniqueness is a two edged sword. According to Lipset, America is the most religious, most optimistic, most patriotic, most rights-oriented and most individualistic country on earth. At the same time, it is the most litigious, has the highest crime rates and the most people incarcerated and the lowest percentage of eligible voters registered to vote of all the developed nations. Similarly, the United States is the wealthiest nation in terms of real income, the most productive as a reflection of worker output with the highest proportion of her population enrolled in higher education. However, it is also "the least egalitarian among developed nations with respect to income distribution, at the bottom as a provider of welfare benefits, the lowest in savings, and the least taxed." Lipset points out that America's uniqueness often appears in baffling contradictions, for example, he finds the US the most moralistic of nations but the nation with the highest crime and divorce rate.[569] What is more according to Lipset, both the good and the bad among American's unique qualities often spring from the same source. For instance, American individualism, with its high sense of personal responsibility and independent initiative, is the driving moral force behind so many Americans political, social, and economic successes. At the same time, it also lies at the heart of American lawlessness, self-indulgence, atomism, and the nation's failure to address social inequities.[570]

All national groups seek to define distinguishing characteristics in order to set themselves off from other nationalities. Belief in national uniqueness is prerequisite to nationalism and to feelings of national superiority. In most nations, distinguishing characteristics include language, religion, skin color, place of origin, or cultural traditions. In this regard, all nations are to some extent unique, however American notions of national uniqueness are rooted in none of

568. Hayes, *Evolution of Modern Nationalism*, 230-1.
569. Lipset, *American Exceptionalism*, 26-7.
570. Lipset, *American Exceptionalism*, 268.

these. In this view, American uniqueness is itself unique. America views itself not only as a unique nation but also as an exceptional nation—"exceptional in the sense of being exemplary, or a beacon among nations; or immune from the social ills and decadence that have beset all other republics in the past; or that it is exempt from the historical course of 'social laws' of development which all nations eventually follow."[571]

Notions of American uniqueness grew out of the consciousness that America was a fusion of peoples, "an asylum for the oppressed."[572] Belief in a national distinctiveness blossomed out of the experience of a diverse people's search for freedom, liberty, equality, and dignity and out of their proof that the masses were competent stewards of government. For Americans, self-rule was the natural right of all mankind, not a privilege bestowed by government. Thus, the unique American identity was ideological in its nature and universal in its scope. America's uniqueness was not defined by ethnic origin, place of origin, or cultural tradition; it was defined by exactly the opposite. For Americans, their nation was unique because it included far-flung ethnicities, myriad cultures, and diverse traditions. It was this "inclusionary focus on universal values" that distinguished American from other nations.[573]

Out of these fundamental universal ideals grew the ideals of American democracy, social elasticity, and laissez-faire capitalism. The success of it all fostered an intense national pride and reinforced a pervasive American individualism, thus further cementing notions of a unique American national identity. Success also brought abundance unlike anything the world had known. It was on the strong shoulders of American plenty that the nation's ideals prospered, and thus, affluence became the "climatic historical source of American uniqueness."[574] When one adds to all of this the unflinching faith in providential destiny and mission that inevitably grows from universal ideologies and a growing identification with the vast homeland of the new continent, the picture of American uniqueness is complete.

Themes of uniqueness lie at both the beginning and the end of all American superiority myths. In order to consider ourselves superior, we must begin by defining ourselves as unique. Conversely, once we define ourselves as superior, themes of uniqueness are expanded and inscribed in stone. The stronger America's sense of uniqueness and superiority becomes, the stronger the potential for alienation from reality.[575]

---

571. Bell, "The 'Hegelian Secret,'" 51.

572. Greenfeld, "American Nationalism," in Krakau, *American Nation*, 37.

573. Greenfeld, "American Nationalism," in Krakau, *American Nation*, 12.

574. Graham, "The Paradox of American Violence," in Graham and Gurr, *Violence in America*, 477.

575. Greenfeld, "American Nationalism," in Krakau, *American Nation*, 40.

The Myth of Anglo-Saxon Superiority

Despite pride in her unique national diversity and her widely perceived notions of unparalleled equality and social flexibility, America was far from the utopian brotherhood she patriotically thought herself to be. From the very beginning of the national epic, the majority of Americans were of Anglo-Saxon descent. While paying lip service to the "melting pot," large parts of this majority held race at the heart of their notions of national superiority and at the center of their worldview. Imported from England in colonial times, the myth of Anglo-Saxon racial supremacy soon inhabited the core of America's self image. The racial traits of both peoples (Americans and English) were defined to include "industry, intelligence, a keen sense of moral purpose, and a talent for government."[576] It was not long before America came to view herself as the heir to British imperial wealth and power. In 1989, Senator Albert Beveridge predicted that the US was destined to become "a greater England with a nobler destiny."[577]

No one knows exactly when the myth of Anglo-Saxon superiority began. It doubtless goes back to the first Angles and Saxons, back to the very beginnings of Teutonic and Aryan peoples in the pre-history of the Asian steps. Whatever its origin, we know that the modern origin of this myth took shape in the nineteenth century as national conflicts raged between Germanic peoples east of the Rhine and Romantic peoples in France. In the last thirty years of the nineteenth century when Franco-Prussian relations began to seriously deteriorate, this myth flourished as a result of the bitter polemic between France and Germany.

As the last decades of the century unfolded, "everywhere the Germanic/Romantic question was given national dimension."[578] In England, the historian Francis Palgrave led the Romantic charge holding that the character of the British Isles had been unscathed by the Anglo-Saxon invasion and that the Norman invasion had further reinforced Romanic traditions in England. On the Germanic side of argument, Edward Freeman, Regius Professor of History at Oxford, argued that British political and social institutions owed their notable success to the Anglo-Saxon influence, which had come to dominate Romantic culture in Great Britain.[579] Freeman published *Comparative Politics* in 1873 proclaiming the superiority of the "Aryan nations" in setting up "constitutional institutions."

> ...[I]n this mighty drama of European and Aryan history, three lands, three races, stand forth before all others, as those to whom, each in its own day, the mission has been given to be the rulers and the teachers of the world.... As the Aryan family of nations, as a whole, stands out above the other families of the world, so the Greek,

---

576. Hunt, *Ideology and US Foreign Policy*, 78.
577. Hunt, *Ideology and US Foreign Policy*, 78.
578. Dementyev, *Imperialist and Anti-imperialist*, 34.
579. Dementyev, *Imperialist and Anti-imperialist*, 33-4.

the Roman, and the Teuton, each in its own turn, stands out above the other nations of the Aryan family.

Freeman zealously promoted his theories of Anglo-Saxon superiority in an American lecture tour in 1881-2, finding an eager audience in a United States.[580]

However, it was not only the English connection that proved the most influential in spreading theories of Aryan, Teutonic, and specifically Anglo-Saxon superiority in America. In the last decades of the nineteenth century, new emphasis and techniques were propelling the study of history to the intellectual forefront in the West, and German scholars were among the first to develop improved methods of historical analysis and advanced techniques in the handling of source materials. Virtually all the prominent American historians of the era studied in Germany. They returned to America with improved German historigraphical methodology and, in many cases, with the Anglo-Saxon superiority myth in tow. Notable in this list is Henry Adams at Harvard, John Burgess at Columbia, Andrew White at Cornell, Charles Adams at the University of Michigan, and Herbert Baxter Adams at Johns Hopkins, who attributed the birth of the principles of individualism and federalism to the tribal system of the Anglo-Saxons. "Montesquieu's winged phrase 'freedom came from the German forests' acquired a new ring on Adams lips."[581] Or as the American historian John Fiske put it in 1885: "In the deepest and widest sense, our American history does not begin with the Declaration of Independence, or even with the settlements at Jamestown and Plymouth; but it descends in unbroken continuity from the days when the stout Arminius in the forests of Northern Germany successfully defied the might of Imperial Rome."[582]

However, the notion that American superiority was born in the forests of Europe ran counter to purely American egoisms. To answer this objection, a new more distinctly American version of the Anglo-Saxon superiority myth emerged. The new myth acknowledged the innate superiority of the Anglo-Saxon peoples who represented the American majority, but it held that in the course of the American experience, this race's dominate superior traits had been watered-down by time and by mixing with the other races and cultures that made up the American minorities. In the new myth, it was the American frontier experience that had honed the mixed immigrant stock to renewed perfection in a crucible that augmented, re-energized, and re-released the dominant Anglo-Saxon supremacy of the American people.

As the theory of Anglo-Saxon superiority gained momentum in America, it was attached to more than just the success of her social and political institutions. Before long it was thought that the unparalleled wit and adaptively Anglo-

---

580. Novick, *That Noble Dream*, 81.
581. Dementyev, *Imperialist and Anti-imperialist*, 34-7.
582. Fiske, *American Political Ideas*, 7.

Saxon leadership also led America to superior economic achievement. As Edward N. Saveth put it:

> The conception of individual liberty, local self-government, freedom from external control which the new historical school claimed to have discovered in the German forests not only provided a basis for the American national character but contributed additional support to a strongly developed philosophy of laissez-faire.... The last stage in the evolution of the heroic Teuton was as the captain of industry, bringing the benefits of 'political organization' to inferior races and resisting the attempts of non-Aryans to fetter his individuality with the chains of socialism.[583]

As the breath of the Anglo-Saxon superiority myth spread to encompass not only political skill, but also economic dexterity and elastic social success, it also gained depth by its association with religious zeal. Notable in this connection is the Rev. Josiah Strong, whose writings and sermons married the force of perceived American Anglo-Saxon superiority to a national mission preordained by God. "Does it not look ... as if God were preparing in our Anglo-Saxon civilization the die with which to stamp the peoples of the earth?" he asked in *Our Country*, his best seller of the 1880s.[584] It was Strong's contention that America was destined to become God's instrument for the regeneration of the world. Inherent in this notion was the conviction of absolute Anglo-Saxon superiority and a strong anti-Catholicism evidenced by the fact that Strong heralded victory in the Spanish American war as both the triumph of the Saxon over the Latin and the Protestant over the Catholic.[585] Strong's writings always linked political and spiritual Anglo-Saxon American superiority. The linkage resulted in the concept of a duel mission: saving both the governments and the souls of all the peoples of the earth.

Such egoism, along with ample helpings of racism and anti-Catholicism, stood at the center of the theory Anglo-Saxon superiority in America, a sweeping theory of preeminence that was confirmed in the popular mind by the perceived unequaled excellence of American political institutions and the incontrovertible conviction of American exclusiveness reflected in the nation's social and economic success.

RACIAL MYTH AND NATIONAL STEREOTYPING

National stereotyping is the logical result of the development of themes of national superiority and uniqueness. The perception of the uniqueness of the nation naturally translates into belief in a kind of mythological national

---

583. Edward N. Saveth, *Political Science Quarterly*, 1939, quoted in Dementyev, *Imperialist and Anti-imperialist*, 38.

584. Strong, *Our Country*, 205.

585. Dementyev, *Imperialist and Anti-imperialist*, 59.

integrity, which is thought to be reflected in the distinctively superior character of the national people. Americans are seen as fiercely independent, self-reliant, innovative, audacious, tenacious, patriotic, earthy, an so on. Over time, these national stereotypes become rhetorically understood and national superiority is taken for granted.

By that time, Americans of light skin, and especially those of English decent, embraced a strict, hierarchal worldview based on skin color. At the top were the superior Anglo-Saxons followed by Germans, who were though to possess many of the same qualities but were also characterized as aggressive, brutal, militaristic, and autocratic. Next came the Slavs, thought to typify hearty peasant stock: rugged enduring, patient, and strong, but lacking in intelligence. Lower down were the Latin peoples of Europe (including the French) who were thought to be sentimental, superstitious, and undisciplined. Farther down were Jews, Asians, and at the very bottom, Africans.[586] Eventually what was originally a myth of Anglo-Saxon superiority was transformed into a myth of American superiority, at least for Americans of Northern European decent. Distinctive, positive, stereotypical American characteristics were eventually perceived to be inborn national inheritances, qualities that describe all Americans and are passed on from generation to generation uncontaminated and un-weakened, almost like genetically transferable traits. In this context, the concept of the nation as a kind of "family" gained new credence, and the national bound was strengthened.

At the same time, notions of stereotypical national traits are also mythologically projected on other nations, who, in contrast to our imagined superior national integrity, are seen to possess negative national characteristics: war-like, inflexible, slow on the uptake, indolent, dirty, and so on. As Michael Hunt observes, "The idea of the Third World has survived sustained by the American conviction of its backwardness and the repressed American consciousness of the color of its peoples."[587]

In America, negative stereotypical themes can be quickly mobilized into support for the national cause by exaggerating the "alien" threat to our national identity, pride, or honor.[588] Thus, American patriotism is easily manipulated, and often sustained on a foundation of untruth. In addition, stereotyping involves more disturbing risks. As Hunt warns, "Denigrating other cultures as backwards or malleable, these stereotypes raise America's false expectations that it is an easy enterprise to induce political and economic development. On encountering obstinacy and resistance, Americans understandably feel frustrated and resentful and in extremity may indulge in dehumanizing stereotypes and make possible resort to forms of violence otherwise unthinkable."[589]

---

586. Hunt, *Ideology and US Foreign Policy*, 78-9.
587. Hunt, *Ideology and US Foreign Policy*, 161-2.
588. Billig, *Banal Nationalism*, 71.

So ingrained and reflexive are these national stereotypes that few of us are conscious of the unrealistic folly of our generalizations. To lump together 250 million people, and categorically label them all "brave" or "thrifty" or "virtuous" would be laughable were it not exactly what we do. Likewise, the tendency to believe stereotypical negative characterizations of "alien" ethnic groups and non-nationals is equally ludicrous and ever more dangerous. To ensure that the fantasy of our glorious national character remains distinct, we exaggerate everything that is thought to distinguish the national group. In manufacturing such distinctions, we strengthen, protect, and preserve the fallacious myths of American superiority and at the same time create an unbridgeable chasm between our nation and the other nations of the world.

---

589. Hunt, *Ideology and US Foreign Policy*, 176.

CHAPTER 13: BLIND FAITH

American notions of superiority and uniqueness embrace a complex set of themes about "us," "our homeland," and the nations of the world ("ours" and "theirs"). As Michael Billig points out, these themes, along with our concepts of national moral duty and national honor, "are widely diffused as common sense."[590] American superiority themes are often invisible to us, because they have so long been taken for granted and routinely infused into ordinary life. American superiority has become part of our assumed national identity. Such blind, unthinking, reflexive nationalism is easily aroused, and Americans are unwittingly vulnerable to blatant manipulations designed to enlist unflinching public support for the United States and her international policies and actions.

All of this not withstanding, the American superiority myth is not solely a product the "American way of life," an egoist national identity, and government propaganda and manipulation; for many it fulfills a fundamental human need.

THE PSYCHOLOGY OF THE MASSES

Notions of American superiority and American vulnerability to transparent public manipulations can be explained in part by recent studies of mass psychology. Modern psychologists see our belief in the uniqueness and superiority of the national character to be the result of a process of identification with the national group in which "the individual ceases to be himself" and seeks to become part of something larger than himself, "something eternal."[591]

---

590. Billig, *Banal Nationalism*, 4.
591. Hoffer, *True Believer*, 63.

According to Erik Hoffer, nationalism affords the individual new pride, confidence and hope as well as a sense of purpose and self-worth through identification with the national cause.[592] At its most fundamental psychological root, it is predisposed by frustration and a loss of faith in the self. Hoffer's is a damning charge: "The less justified a man is in claiming excellence in himself, the more ready he is to claim excellence for his nation."[593]

The ramifications of such an idea are beyond the scope of this book, but whatever the cause, our belief in the superiority of the national cause often borders on fanaticism. Here Hoffer's characterization of the "true believer" has a distinctly American ring: "The true believer is apt to see himself as one of the chosen, ... the light of the world."[594] According to Hoffer, "All mass movements strive ... to interpose a fact-proof screen between the faithful and the realities of the world. They do this by claiming that the ultimate and absolute truth is already in their doctrine and that there is no truth or certitude outside it."[595] As Deborah Madsen puts it, "Exceptionalism has always offered a mythological refuge from the chaos of history and the uncertainties of life."[596]

In attempting to penetrate the collective American mind, Paul Wachtel finds it useful to examine individual strategies for building personal security and then apply them to the national psyche at large. Employing terms developed by Karen Horney, Wachtel contends that America is "caught put in a societal 'moving-against' neurosis." Horney defines three separate strategies that individuals employ to build personal security: "moving-toward" in which the subject attempts to bind himself to others by being meek, agreeable, nice etc.; "moving-against" in which the subject "attempts to ward off feelings of weakness and vulnerability by striving to be successful, admired and in charge;" and "moving away," a strategy by which the subject tries to avoid any meaningful ties.[597]

According to Wachtel, "the 'moving against' neurotic trend captures something important about the manifest patterns of behavior that most characterize our public life and the workings of our economic system."[598] Like "moving-against" individuals, America collectively values being "tough, strong, hard-headed and dynamic." For Wachtel, superior "skill, strength, and success" are the currency and sources of our national self-esteem.[599]

---

592. Hoffer, *True Believer*, 12.

593. Hoffer, *True Believer*, 14.

594. Hoffer, *True Believer*, 97-8.

595. Hoffer, *True Believer*, 78.

596. Masden, *American Exceptionalism*, 166.

597. Karner Horney, *Neurotic Personality of Our Time*, cited in Wachtel, *Poverty of Affluence*, 70-3.

598. Wachtel, *Poverty of Affluence*, 78.

599. Wachtel, *Poverty of Affluence*, 71-2, 78.

UNIVERSALISM, NATIONALISM, AND PATRIOTISM

Inherent in the notion of America's faith in her doctrine of "absolute truth" is the belief that American interests represent the interest of the world, that America stands for all of mankind, that we act on behalf of "the universal order of nations" for the good of the "universal audience of humanity."[600] America has always defined herself as "a great experiment for the demonstration of higher purposes,"[601] a defender of universal moral right. Thus, nations that oppose us are *de facto* demonic, naturally viewed as enemies of international progress and threats to the moral order of the world. If we represent the one universal Truth, then our enemies naturally become the universal enemy.[602]

Accordingly, our nationalism is seen as the rational, "benevolent sort," and the nationalism of our enemies is viewed as dangerously irrational and selfish. Indeed, the very word "nationalism" itself seems to run counter to the American universal ideal. Thus, Americans compound their self-deception by re-labeling American nationalism, "patriotism." "We" are patriots. "They" are nationalists. The difference between a nationalist and a patriot is a matter of his priorities. Both love their country, but the nationalist places his love of country above all other values, even above his love of humanity. Herein lies the central paradox of American "patriotism:" if our national cause is the salvation of all other nations, then we must place our nation's cause above those of all other nations. If we do that, then we are no longer patriots, we are nationalists despite our good intentions.

Considerable self-deception is required to reconcile such a conundrum. We must become blind to our own fanaticism. We must attach "our patriotism" to categorical goodness, and "their nationalism" to categorical evil. There can be no shades of gray, lest we reveal the paradox and discover the unbending true fundamentalism of our own unlovely nationalism.

> "The wars waged by US troops; the bombings in Vietnam and Iraq; the bombasity of US presidents; and the endless display of the revered flag; all of these are removed from the problems of over-heated nationalism" and "transmuted into the warm glow of patriotism, the healthy necessity rather than the dangerous surplus."[603]

---

600. Billig, *Banal Nationalism*, 89.
601. Stephanson, *Manifest Destiny*, 21.
602. Billig, *Banal Nationalism*, 92.
603. Billig, *Banal Nationalism*, 56.

PART FOUR: TOLERANCE AND PLURALITY

Chapter 14: In Search of American Humility

The term "American humility" is rare indeed. For most, it appears as an oxymoron. One might argue that in order to temper America's runaway superiority complex, an appeal to "American tolerance" would be more apt. This is true, however, no genuine tolerance can be achieved without proper grounding in humility.

Humility in this context is not intended to suggest a zealous, self-flagellating, humbling of the national spirit. Nor is it intended to imply American deference or submission. Rather it is employed only to suggest the opposite of American arrogance. Here an appeal to "American humility" is simply a call for that modest pride in national achievements and institutions that is mediated by the realization that we live in an increasingly pluralistic world, and that no one nation, no one culture, no one people have all the answers to an increasingly complex human universe.

Humility and Ideology

In the harsh light of today's fragmenting world, an appeal to national humility appears reasonable enough. However, any semblance of American humility will require sweeping changes in American thought, a radical and fundamental shift in the very foundations of the American national identity. Concepts of liberty, individualism, democracy, capitalism, equality, and social elasticity still quite literally define what it means to be an American. Since the United States of America is a nation held together by an unflinchingly absolute ideology perceived as a universal truth, in the American mind the idea that other social, political, and economic solutions might be alternatively or simultaneously valid in some situations or in some parts of the world, constitutes, not just ideological blasphemy, but a serious threat to the nation. All variant ideologies are viewed as threats, not just to our ideology, but to the integrity and binding fabric of our nation, and any notion that American ideals are not necessarily universal truths appears equally threatening.

Thus, it is out of a desperate sense of self-preservation that America nurtures her notions of universal superiority and remains blind to the central fact of the emerging postmodern world: that "everything — communications, the economy, our sense of time and space, science, the new humanism — indicate variety and not monotony, diversity and not unity, alternatively and not identity, the polytheism of rather than the monotheism of values."[604] Thus, it is that Americans are incapable of humility.

Such a flaw is typical of nationalist nations. Nationalists, with their unflinching, elitist devotion to the perceived national interest, are by definition incapable of ideological humility. Despite the freedoms American nationalists purport to defend, they are chauvinistic and intolerant of dissent, insisting on a nearly totalitarian rigidity of belief. As Ernest Geller reminds us, "nationalism makes for homogeneity of a single high culture within the political unit, which condemns those not masters of said culture."[605]

None of this is intended to imply that American ideals are suspect. They are fine and noble. Their evolution and practice represents a quantum leap in the evolution of mankind of which Americans can be justly proud. What *is* implied here is that American ideals are part of a process. They are neither absolute nor universal. They are simply steps in mankind's evolutionary journey toward the goal of equality and the universal good. They are not the final, perfect realization of that journey.

Acceptance of the notion that American ideals are a step in an on-going universal progress would suggest not only hopeful openness and tolerance, but also a certain measured humility, along with an appropriately modest sense of national pride. However, American ideology has always rested on seemingly common sense notions of universality. In the American mind such universality is not incremental, rather it represents an accomplished whole, a consummate ultimate truth. American ideology thus allows no room for plurality, humility or tolerance. Ironically, the nation that fights and dies for free speech, free ideas, and free thought, remains totally closed to and threatened by any ideology save its own.

---

604. Max Weber quoted in Fuentes, Prologue to *Ariel* by Rodó, trans. Paden, 19.
605. Geller, *Nationalism*, 103.

HUMILITY AND PLURALISM

Arrogant notions of superiority are inherent in a nation that views itself to be in sole possession of ultimate truth. Despite the fragmenting world we see all around us, American policy revolves around a single system of interpretation. As Arthur Schlesinger Jr. observes, the real world conflict today is "between those who would reduce the world to one and those who see it as many — between those who believe that the world is evolving toward a single direction ... and those who think humanity will evolve along diverse paths."[606]

Evidence of the plural nature of the modern world is everywhere. Human diversity seems more overwhelming every day, and yet, Americans remain blind to it. The grand meta-narratives, which established clear boundaries between truth and falsity belong to the modernist past. The post-modern world is seen by many as ill-defined and evolving. Nevertheless, it appears real enough to make it too late for us to be for or against postmodernism. Globalization, fragmentation, variety, and uncertainty are facts of life, and it now appears clear that science and reason have not, and will not, produce any clear unambiguous ultimate truths.

Still, there are lingering problems with postmodernism. Theoretically, in a postmodern world nationalism should be declining, giving way to the eroding of the nation-state by globalization from without and the rise of regional and local movements from within. Theoretically, the postmodern world should be characterized by "supra-national" or "intra-national" or even "infra-national" factions.[607] Strangely, this is not the case so far. The bounded homeland and the bold distinctions between "us" and "them" remain very real. As Michael Billig sees it, "The habits of past thinking persist, ... they are rooted in forms of life, in an era in which the state may be changing, but has not yet withered away."[608]

Still the handwriting is on the wall. Although nationalist notions of superiority stubbornly refuse to loosen their grip on the American psyche, the globalization of capital is fast becoming a reality, and myths of American economic superiority are beginning to unravel. Perhaps the business of America is still business, but in the postmodern world, business will know no nationality. Americans find this impossible to grasp, just as they found Sputnik unimaginable. How could it be that any other nation could "beat" us in a technological contest? After Sputnik, the "space race" took on a character that had little to do with scientific research. America was determined to prove her superiority, and so she did what she always does when faced with a problem, she threw money at it. Thirty years later, it might have been acceptable for Europeans to make better

---

606. Schlesinger Jr., "One Against the Many," in Schlesinger Jr. and White, *Paths of American Thought*, 537.
607. Billig, *Banal Nationalism*, 140.
608. Billig, *Banal Nationalism*, 139.

luxury cars, but the mass produced popular automobile still appeared to be as American as Henry Ford; that is until the Japanese began to produce far superior, far less costly, far more durable cars for the world market place. America automakers are still trying to catch up. Meanwhile the European aviation industry competes head up with Boeing and McDonald Douglas. The European Union is just beginning to vie with America for world economic preeminence, the euro is fast replacing the American dollar as the worlds benchmark currency, and the sleeping giants of China and southern Asia are starting to stir. All of this is unfathomable to Americans, who cling to ingrained notions of economic superiority, despite all indications to the contrary. America has her head in the sand; she blindly considers serious foreign competition for world markets to be impossible, when it is actually inevitable, when it is just another indication of the multifoliate possibilities inherent in a pluralistic world.

America must reinvent itself. Happily, the process will not require reinventing American ideology, which is noble and fine, although badly in need of some maintenance and care. It will however, require rethinking notions of American superiority, tempering the idea that American ideology constitutes a universal truth, and putting aside national fears that variant ideologies constitute a threat to the nation. At its core, the world, when left alone, is not anti-American, it is just itself.[609] However, America cannot seem to leave the world alone, and her compulsive manipulations, although undertaken in the name of liberty and democracy, are often seen as transparent attempts to oblige her obsession with "national security," and are thus the source of bitter hostility abroad. America must begin to accept the pluralistic fate of the world, and a measure of humility is required for such an acceptance.

We are a nation captive in a prison of our own making. The United States of American was founded on noble principles that were deemed to spring from "natural rights." This is what binds the nation together, the idea that our rights as citizens are derived not from the fact that we are Americans, but from the fact that we are human. For Americans, it is a seemingly logical jump to the universal imperative of such ideals. This is how American interventionist policy is justified in the national consciousness, but the rest of the world does not necessarily see it that way. As Liah Greenfeld puts it, "To be an American means to persevere in one's loyalty to these ideals, in spite of the inescapable contradictions between them and reality."[610]

America, like all nations, must pass from nationalism to inter-dependence. However, in so doing, we must realize that this path is difficult for other nations as well, especially those who are yet to know independence. As Carlos Fuentes warns, "inter-dependence is senseless without a basis in independence. Only independent nations can become inter-dependent partners."[611] The task at hand

---

609. Fuentes, Prologue to *Ariel* by Rodó, trans. Paden, 24.
610. Greenfeld, "American Nationalism," in Krakau, *American Nation*, 50.

is twofold: to preserve national identity *and* to test the waters of alternatively. So far, this challenge has appeared to represent an irreconcilable contradiction for the United States.

TOWARD AMERICAN CULTURAL HUMILITY

Let us now return to the point at which we began, the Uruguayan author, José Enrique Rodó, and his insightful, turn-of-the-century essay, *Ariel*, the emotional, intellectual and spiritual Latin American response to growing North American arrogance. Rodó paints a highly polarized picture of a world characterized by simplistic dualisms: spirit versus utility, beauty versus ugliness, delicateness versus vulgarity, good versus evil.[612] His assessment of the United States, although perhaps overly generalized, is penetrating and, at least so far, appears timeless. The probing depth of Rodó's insight stems from the fact that his criticism of America is not just political, social, and economic, but also cultural. Rodó believes that the intrinsic values of a society, not the values of its institutions, are the superior measures of national worth. By this yardstick, he finds the United States wanting. Great civilizations, he contends, acquire their character not from power and material prosperity, but from the "grandeur of their thought and feelings possible within it."[613]

Rodó describes American culture at the turn of the twentieth century as an "empire of mediocrity" which has erected "barriers to higher culture."[614] In examining the great North American democracy, *Ariel* points to a "tyranny of the masses," having effected a kind of social leveling that has thwarted superior intellect and deprived the nation of moral leadership. Rodó argues that in the United States, the "leveling of the middle class" has tended to "plane down what little there remains of the intelligentsia."[615] Thus for Rodó the United States lacks the proper cultural underpinnings to sustain itself; or as Carlos Fuentes so aptly puts it in his Prologue to the new translation of *Ariel*, Rodó fears that the superpowers are powerful "only because they are heavily armed."[616] In 1900 Rodó wrote, "The North American has not yet replaced the inspiring ideality of his past with any high, unselfish conception of the future. He lives for the immediate reality of the present, and for this subordinates all of his activities in the egoism of material well-being."[617] Over a hundred years later, in attempting to

611. Fuentes, Prologue to *Ariel* by Rodó, trans. Paden, 18.
612. Fuentes, Prologue to *Ariel* by Rodó, trans. Paden, 14.
613. Rodó, *Ariel*, Trans. Stinson.
614. Rodó, *Ariel*, Trans. Stinson, 63-4.
615. Rodó, *Ariel*, Trans. Stinson, 113.
616. Fuentes, Prologue to *Ariel* by Rodó, trans. Paden, 23.
617. Rodó, *Ariel*, trans. Stinson, 107.

voice the current view of the United States from abroad, the American scholar Anthony Judt would write, "The US is a selfish, individualistic society devoted to commerce, profit, and the despoliation of the planet. It is uncaring of the poor and sick, and it is indifferent to the rest of humankind."[618] By this measure, today it appears that Rodó's criticism of the United States has stood the muster of time.

In the present world-metamorphosis of the internationalization of capital, the transitional world-culture is decidedly American. However, in much of the turbulent modern world, the contemporary image of the United States is that of a "decadent, voracious" giant, standardizing, dehumanizing, and homogenizing everything it touches. "Cash is the measure of worth, quantity is a value." Today, despite its many attractions, America is often viewed as a nation inflicted with incurable and highly contagious economic and moral diseases.[619] Meanwhile, Europe has again come to view itself as the "repository of a precious civilization ... assaulted by transatlantic barbarism."[620]

Needless to say, America does not see it that way. According to the American view, at the end of the Second World War, the United States sought to take up the torch of Western culture, which had been dropped by Europe, and to point all of the world toward a better way. Americans still revel in the unprecedented national benevolence that begot the Marshall Plan and the donation of the equivalent of hundreds of billions of today's dollars to Europe's victors and vanquished alike. This, along with the reconstruction of war-shattered Japan, is still the source of blind nation pride, even though its motivation was not wholly altruistic, in as much as it assured "bought-and-paid-for," "made-in-America cooperation" against the spread of communism. [621]

On the other side of the Atlantic today, the Marshall Plan is ancient history, and it is clear that many modern Europeans today have come to find American arrogance repugnant a number of ways. Once the exclusive pastime of the European elite, America-bashing has today become widespread on the continent, and the list of charges continues to grow. Ranking high on this list are overt displays of flag-waving American patriotism, which most European view with lofty disdain. Also near the top of the list is the seemingly obligatory American zeal that points to a national epidemic of over-competitiveness that is especially evident at sporting events where chants of "USA, USA" and "We're number one," grate of the European sense of decorum and modesty. Certainly, examples of the hollowness of American consumerism and pop culture also pop-

618. Judt, "It's the American Way," in *Financial Review*, April, 2003.
619. Cunliffe, "European Images of America," in Schlesinger Jr. and White, *Paths of American Thought*, 506.
620. Cunliffe, "European Images of America," in Schlesinger Jr. and White, *Paths of American Thought*, 506.
621. Reid, *United States of Europe*, 39.

ulate the list, although it appears that most European are every bit as eager as the Americans to soak up this vapid, media-driven pap. On more substantial issues, the majority of Europeans are appalled by American gun control, or lack of it, and by what they perceive as the utter barbarity of a nation that still clings to the death penalty. In general, Europeans are more disposed to social democracy and America's dedication to passive laissez-faire mechanisms rather than active governmental remedies for social inequities appear to most observers on the continent be callous and insensitive to the needs of the poor.

In the European eye, perhaps the most damning characteristic of America is her unapologetic provincialism. In general, Americans appear to have no understanding of, or interest in, foreign culture, languages, customs, or beliefs. In *The United States of Europe*, T. R. Reid aptly quotes the nineteenth-century British traveler Frances Trollope in this connection:

> If the citizens of the United States were indeed the devoted patriots they call themselves, they would surely not thus encrust themselves in the hard, dry, stubborn persuasion that they are the first and the best of the human race, that nothing is to be learnt, but what they are able to teach, and that nothing is worth having, which they do not possess.

In more contemporary terms, Brian Reade writes that Americans are a "people who believe that the world stretches from California to Boston."[622]

In the European mind, such a provincial mindset constitutes a fearful combination of strength and stupidity. In the words of the French parliamentarian Noel Mamere, "Omnipotence and ignorance is a questionable cocktail. It would be great if they [the Americans] saw what they looked like from over here. But they are not interested. They think that they are the best in the world, that they are way ahead of everyone, and everyone needs to learn from them."[623] Reid insists that most Europeans have ceased to view the US as protector and now view it as a threat. This, according to Reid, is one of the primary reasons for the ongoing strengthening of the European Union. "Since the Europeans no can longer trust or align themselves with the world's only superpower, they have no choice but to build a superpower of their own."[624] Again Anthony Judt summaries the European view of America well:

> The US rides roughshod over international laws and treaties and the moral, environmental, and physical future of humanity. It is inconsistent and hypocritical in its foreign dealings, and it wields unparalleled military clout. It is, in short, a bull in the global china shop.[625]

---

622. Ried, *United States of Europe*, 7-19; Trollope, *Domestic Manners of Americans*, 1852, quoted in Reid, *United States of Europe*, 18; Brian Reade in The London *Mirror*, quoted in Reid, *United States of Europe*, 18.

623. Mamere, *No, Thanks, Uncle Sam*, quoted in Reid, *United States of Europe*, 19.

624. Ried, *United States of Europe*, 24.

625. Judt, "It's the American Way," in *Financial Review*, April, 2003.

Sadly, in the case of Europe, hostility toward the United States goes far deeper than issues of foreign policy, conflicting domestic practices, or cultural conventions. Deeply fundamental ideological issues are emerging to which the United States continues to turn an egotistically blind eye. America refuses to accept the fact that the one thing she holds most dear, her so-called "American way," that "unique mix of moralistic religiosity, minimal provisions for public welfare and maximal market freedom ... coupled with a missionary foreign policy ostensibly directed at exporting the same cluster of values and practices" is precisely what the Europeans find so unpalatable.[626] More and more Europe favors a social democracy in which some liberty is sacrificed to the common humanitarian good, while America becomes more insistent that, with minimal governmental interference, liberty is self-regulating. At the bottom of it all, lies America's arrogant indifference to this growing divergence of ideologies, a national indifference fostered by the unfathomably monolithic nature of her political culture. That is what Europeans really finds so abhorrent.

The current anti-Americanism in Europe goes well beyond the perception of wrong-minded US policies. According to the Lithuanian scholar Algirdas Degutis, "It is a blanket rejection of anything the United States does at any place and time." Degutis describes an atmosphere of "animosity and suspicion" in which the US is seen as a "global predator." "The discourse," he reports, "is not merely critical; it is one of total damnation. The target of the critique is beyond redemption."[627] None of this is new. Writing in 1995, Paul Hollander painted a disturbing portrait of the evolving European bias. According to Hollander, modern anti-Americanism denotes "a particular mindset, an attitude of distaste, aversion, or intense hostility the roots of which may be found in matters unrelated to the actual qualities or attributes of American society or the foreign policies of the Unites States. In short, anti-Americanism refers to a negative predisposition, a type of bias, which is to various degrees unfounded.... [It is] an attitude similar to [such other] hostile dispositions as racism, sexism, and anti-Semitism."[628] What is more, most observers agree that anti-American sentiment in Europe is no longer the exclusive domain of the intellectual community, but "is widespread, rising, and migrating from its traditional home among left-wing intellectuals, academics and café society to the political mainstream."[629]

So it is that the view of America from abroad at the beginning of the twenty-first century has changed little since the beginning of the twentieth. In 1900, Rodó saw the United States as unworthy of imitation, and, although he feared growing American world power, he had a deeper reason to eschew imi-

626. Judt, "It's the American Way," *Financial Review*, April, 2003.
627. Degutis, "American Threat."
628. Hollander, *Anti-Americanism*, lxxviii, quoted in Degutis, "American Threat."
629. Frankel, "Anti-Americanism Moves to W. Europe's Mainstream," *Washington Post*, February 11, 2003, A1, quoted in Degutis, "American Threat."

tation. Imitation, Rodó wrote, "denaturalizes the character of the people," robbing them of their "personal genius," which once lost can never be replaced.[630] "If one can dimly foresee the higher concord of the future," he writes, it will not reflect "the one-sided imitation of one race by the other," but rather the "reciprocity of those attitudes which make the peculiar glory of either race."[631]

In this quest for Latin American identity, Rodó thus rejects the emulation of both North American and European models in favor of a "cosmopolitanism which conciliates national identity and universal values of wholeness."[632] In short, Rodó is acknowledging a pluralistic world-view, "seeing that nature has more than one face, that humans have a variety of ideas and interests."[633] In 1900, such an idea foreshadowed postmodern theory and the ideas of the many modern thinkers who later began to celebrate alternatives and to view the widespread fragmentation of values as a value in itself.[634] In his prologue to the new English translation of *Ariel*, Carlos Fuentes notes Rodó's foresight:

> Rodó unwittingly announces an era of political and cultural diversification, best explained by the Spanish philosopher Ortega y Gasset, when, in his *Theory of Andalusia*, he writes that "life is first of all an ensemble of problems to which we answer with an ensemble of solutions called culture," but "since many solutions are possible" it follows that a plurality of cultures have existed and shall exist. "What has never existed," concludes Ortega y Gasset, "is an absolute culture, that is, a culture responding successfully to every objection."[635]

> We have learned during our cruel century that, since there is no absolute culture, there can be no absolute politics. What exists are many cultures — many truths — expressing themselves through many kinds of politics.[636]

In 1900, Rodó feared that the power and influence of the United States was "effecting a kind of moral conquest."[637] Thus, Rodó's vision of the emerging Latin America identity was not at all like the inflexible superiority of the US self-image. It was, and is, a dream of many ideologies, many cultures, many truths. It is a realistically humble dream that Americans would do well to carefully consider.

Over her short history as a nation, America's convictions of national superiority, nationalism, and xenophobia have become part of the national common

---

630. Rodó, *Ariel*, trans. Stinson, 92.
631. Rodó, *Ariel*, trans. Stinson, 95.
632. Fuentes, Prologue to *Ariel* by Rodó, trans. Paden, 18.
633. Rodó, *Ariel*, trans. Paden.
634. Bakhtin, Adorno, Weber for example in Fuentes, Prologue to *Ariel* by Rodó, trans. Paden, 19.
635. Ortega y Gasset, *The Theory of Andalusia* in Fuentes, Prologue to *Ariel* by Rodó, trans. Paden, 23.
636. Fuentes, Prologue to *Ariel* by Rodó, trans. Paden, 23.
637. Rodó, *Ariel*, trans. Paden.

sense. We have become blind to our growing national egoism, developed irrational fears, and lost our noble sense of national direction. Words like "liberty" and "democracy" have been stripped of their original implications, and enlisted as emotional banners employed to inspire nationalism's zealot multitudes.

In order to find the inner-peace that can only come from a comfortable sense of national humility, Americans must first come to understand the roots of their deep seeded notions of national superiority and unmask the myths and manipulations that have turned patriotism into elitist nationalism. Until the United States can put aside her fearful notions regarding ideologies, societies, and cultures different from her own and cease her audacious, thinly disguised quest for hegemony, her pretensions to global moral leadership will remain a mockery in the eyes of the rest of the world.

BIBLIOGRAPHY

Adams, Charles Francis. *Imperialism and the Tracks of Our Forefathers.* Boston: 1895

Adler, Selig. *The Isolationist Impulse: Its Twentieth Century Reaction.* London and New York: Abelard-Schuman Limited, 1957.

Anderson, Benedict. *Imagined Communities: Reflections on the Origins and Spread of Nationalism.* Revised Edition. London and New York: Verso, 1991.

Arieli, Yehoshua. *Individualism and Nationalism in American Ideology.* 1964: Reprint, Baltimore: Penguin Books, 1966.

——— "Individualism and National Identity." In Curry and Goodheart, eds., *American Chameleon, Individualism in Trans-national Context.*

Bacon, Francis. "New Atlantis." In Morley, *Ideal Commonwealths.* London: 1901.

Baudet, Henri. *Paradise on Earth: Some Thoughts on European Images of Non-European Man.* New Haven: Yale University Press, 1965.

Baritz, Loren. "God's Country and American Know-How." In Davis and Woodman, *Conflict and Consensus,* 470-483.

Bell, Daniel. "The 'Hegelian Secret': Civil Society and American Exceptionalism." In Shafer, *Is American Different?.*

Bercovitch, Sacvan. *The Rites of Assent: Transformation in the Symbolic Construction of America.* New York: Routledge, 1993.

Bhabha, Homi K. ed. *Nation and Narrative.* London and New York: Rutledge, 1990.

Billig, Michael. *Banal Nationalism.* London, Thousand Oaks, New Delhi: SAGE Publications, 1995.

Birch, Anthony Harold. *Nationalism and National Integration.* London: Unwin Hyman, 1989.

Bliss, Howard, and M. Glen Johnson, "The Agonizing Reappraisal: Origins of the Cold War." In Bliss and Johnson, *Consensus at the Crossroads.*

———— "The Containment Doctrine and the Rise of American Globalism." In Bliss and Johnson, *Consensus at the Crossroads.*

———— ed. *Consensus at the Crossroads: Dialogues in American Foreign Policy.* New York and Toronto: Dobb, Mead & Company, 1972.

Bloom, Allan, *The Closing of the American Mind: How Higher Education has Failed Democracy and Impoverish the Souls of Today's Students.* New York: Simon and Schuster, 1987.

Brennan, Timothy. "The National Longing for Form." In Bhabha, *Nation and Narrative.*

Bronowski, Jacob and Bruce Mazlish. *The Western Intellectual Tradition form Leonardo to Hegel.* 1960. New York: Harper & Row, Publishers, 1962.

Brown, Richard Maxwell. "Historical Patterns of American Violence." In Graham and Gurr, *Violence in America.*

Bryant, William Jennings, et. al. *Republic or Empire: The Philippine Question.* Chicago, n.p. 1899, 83.

Bryce, James. "The Tyranny of the Multitude." In Rapson, *Individualism and Conformity.*

Bundy, McGeorge, "Foreign Policy: From Innocence to Engagement." In Schlesinger Jr. and Morton, *Paths of American Thought*, 293-308.

Burgess, John William. "The Ideal of the American Commonwealth." In *Political Science Quarterly*, Vol. X, No. 1, September 1895.

Burke, Edmund. *Selected Works*, Oxford: Clarendon Press, 1904.

Burke, Joseph H. *The Tyranny of Malice: Exploring the Dark Side of Character and Culture.* New York and London: Summit Books, 1988.

Cahoone, Lawrence, ed. *Modernism to Postmodernism: An Anthology.* Second Edition. Malden, MA: Blackwell Publishing Ltd., 2003.

Chevalier, Michael. *Society, Manners and Politics in the United States.* Boston, 1839.

Cocks, Joan. *Passion and Paradox: Intellectuals Confront the National Question.* Princeton and Oxford: Princeton University Press, 2002.

Commager, Henry Steele. *The American Mind: An Interpretation of American Thought and Character Since 1880.* New Haven: Yale University Press, 1950.

———— "The History of American Violence: An Interpretation." In Graham, *Violence: The Crisis of American Confidence.*

Crichfield, George W. *American Supremacy: The Rise and Progress of the Latin American Republics and Their Relations to the United States Under the Monroe Doctrine.* 2 vols. New York: Brentano's, 1908.

Cunliffe, Marcus. "European Images of America." In Schlesinger Jr. and Morton, *Paths of American Thought*, 492-514.

Curran, Thomas J. *Xenophobia and Immigration: 1880-1930*. Boston: Twayne Publications, 1975.

Curry, Richard O. and Lawrence B. Goodheart, eds. *American Chameleon, Individualism in Trans-national Context*. Kent, OH and London: The Kent State University Press, 1991

Davis, Allen F. and Harold D. Woodman, ed. *Conflict and Consensus in Modern American History. Lexington*, MA: D C. Heath and Company, 1988.

Davis, J. C. *Utopia and the Ideal Society: A Study of English Utopian Writing, 1516-1700*. Cambridge, Cambridge University Press, 1981.

Degutis, Algirdas. "The American Threat as Perceived by Europeans." Paper Presented at COST Action 24 WG2 and WG3 Seminars, The Evolving Social Construction of Threats, September 20 –21, 2004, Brussels. http://www.cost.a24.info/images/stories/documents/2004-sept-algirdas%20degutis%2020.

Dementyev, I. *Imperialist and Anti-Imperialist: The Great Policy Debate at the Turn of the Century*. Translated by David Skvirsky. Moscow: Progress Publishers, 1979.

Divine, Robert A. *The Reluctant Belligerent: American Entry into World War II*. New York, London, and Sidney: John Wiley and Sons, 1965.

Dudden, Arthur P., ed. *Woodrow Wilson and the World Today*. Philadelphia: University of Pennsylvania Press, 1957.

Elliot, J. H. *The Old World and the New 1492-1650*. Cambridge: Cambridge University Press, 1970.

Emerson, Ralph Waldo. *The Complete Writings of Ralph Waldo Emerson: Containing All His Essays, Poems, Lectures*..... 8 vols. New York: William H. Wise and Company, 1929.

Ergang, Robert. *Europe: From the Renaissance to Waterloo*. 1939, Boston: D. C. Heath, 1954.

Evans, Harold. *They Made America*. New York: Little, Brown and Company, 2004.

Fiske, John. *American Political Ideas Viewed from the Standpoint of Universal History: Three Lectures Delivered at the Royal Institution of Great Britain in May of 1880*. New York: Harper and Brothers, 1885.

Fuentes, Carlos. Prologue to *Ariel*, by José Enrique Rodó. Translated by Margaret Sayers Paden. Austin: University of Texas Press, 1988.

Fukuyama, Francis. "The West May be Cracking: America vs. the Rest," New Perspective Quarterly. Vol. 21, No. 3. Summer 2004.

Fulbright, J. William. *The Arrogance of Power*. New York: Random House, 1966.

———"The Arrogance of Power." In Bliss and Johnson, *Consensus at the Crossroads*.

Furay, Conal, *The Grass-roots Mind in America: The American Sense of Absolutes*. New York and London: New Viewpoints, 1977.

Gellner, Ernest. *Nationalism*. London: Weidenfeld and Nicolson, 1997.

——— *Thought and Change*. London: Weidenfeld and Nicolson, 1964.

Gibson, James William. "American Paramilitary Culture and the Reconstitution of the Vietnam War." In Walsh and Aulich, *Vietnam Images*, 1989.

Giddens, Anthony. *Social Theory and Modern Sociology.* Cambridge: Polity Press, 1987.

————*The Nation-state and Violence*, Cambridge, Polity Press, 1985.

Goebel, Thomas. "A Government of Laws or a Government of People? Direct Democracy and American Political Culture, 1890-1920." In Krakau, *American Nation, National Identity, Nationalism*, 123-148.

Graham, Hugh Davis, ed. *Violence: The Crisis of American Confidence.* Baltimore and London: Johns Hopkins Press, 1971.

———— "The Paradox of American Violence." In Graham and Gurr, *Violence in America*.

Graham, Hugh Davis, and Ted Robert Gurr, ed. *Violence in America: Historical and Comparative Perspective.* Revised Edition. Beverly Hills and London: Sage Publications, 1979.

Greene, Jack P. *The Intellectual Construction of America: Exceptionalism and Identity from 1492 to 1800.* Chapel Hill: University of North Carolina Press, 1993.

Greene, Theodore P. *American Imperialism in 1898.* Boston: Heath, 1955.

Greenfeld, Liah. *Nationalism: Five Roads to Modernity.* Cambridge, MA: Harvard University Press, 1992.

————"The Origins and Nature of American Nationalism in Comparative Perspective." In Krakau, *American Nation, National Identity, Nationalism*, 19-52.

Gutfeld, Arnon, *American Exceptionalism: The Effects of Plenty in the American Experience.* Brighton and Portland: Suddex Academic Press, 2002.

Hacker, Louis M. *The Triumph of American Capitalism: The Development of Forces in American History to the End of the Nineteenth Century.* New York, Columbia University Press,1940.

Hayes, Carlton J. *The Historical Evolution of Modern Nationalism.* 1931. Reprint, New York: Russell & Russell, 1968.

Healy, David. US *Expansionism: The Imperialist Urge in the 1890s.* Madison, WI: University of Wisconsin Press, 1970.

Hindle, Brooke. *Technology in Early America: Needs and Opportunities for Study.* Chapel Hill, NC: University of North Carolina Press, 1966.

Hockenos, Paul. *Free to Hate: The Rise of the Right in Post Communist Europe.* New York and London: Routledge, 1993.

Hoffer, Eric. *The True Believer: Thoughts of the Nature of Mass Movements.* New York and Evanston: Harper & Row Publishers, 1951.

Hofstadter, Richard. *Social Darwinism in American Thought.* 1944. Boston: Beacon Press, 1962.

Hollander, Paul. *Anti-Americanism: Irrational and Rational.* Piscataway, NJ: Transaction Publishers, 1995.

Horney, Karen. *The Neurotic Personality of Our Time*. New York: Norton, 1937.

Hughes, Thomas P. *American Genius: A Century of Invention and Technological Enthusiasm, 1870-1970*. New York: Viking, 1989.

Hunt, Michael H. *Ideology and US Foreign Policy*. New Haven and New York: Yale University Press, 1987.

Jefferson, Thomas. *The Writings of Thomas Jefferson*, 20 vols. Memorial Edition. Washington, D. C: The Thomas Jefferson Memorial Association of the United States, Lipscomb, 1904-05.

Jennings, Francis. *The Invasion of America: Indians, Colonialism and the Cant of Conquest*. Chapel Hill: University of North Carolina Press, 1975.

Jones, Howard Mumford. *O Strange New World: American Culture, The Formative Years*. New York: Viking, 1964.

Judt, Anthony. "It's the American Way." In *Financial Review*, April, 2003.

Kecmanovic, Dusan. *The Psychology of Ethenonationalism*. New York and London: Plenum Press, 1996.

Kent, James. *Dissertations: Being the Preliminary Part of a Course of Law Lectures*. New York: 1795.

Kidd, Benjamin. *Control of the Tropics*. Boston: n.p., 1898.

Kipling, Rudyard. *Collected Verse of Rudyard Kipling*. Garden City, NY: Doubleday, Page and Company, 1915.

Krakau, Kund, "Nation — National Identity — Nationalism: An Introduction." In Krakau, *American Nation, National Identity, Nationalism*, 7-16.

——— ed, *The American Nation, National Identity, Nationalism*. Munster: Lit Verlag, 1997.

Langer, William L. "Peace and the New Order." In Dudden, *Woodrow Wilson and the World Today*.

Lasky, Melvin J. "America and Europe: Transatlantic Images." In Schlesinger Jr. and Morton, *Paths of American Thought*, 465-491.

Lerner, Max. "The Triumph of Laissez-faire." In Schlesinger Jr. and White, *Paths of American Thought*, 147-166.

Lewis, R. W. B. *The American Adam*, Chicago: University of Chicago Press, 1959.

Lipset, Seymour Martin. *American Exceptionalism: A Double Edged Sword*. New York: W. W. Norton and Company, 1996.

——— "American Exceptionalism Reaffirmed." In Shafer, *Is American Different?*.

Limerick, Patricia Nelson. *The Legacy of Conquest: The Unbroken Past of the American West*. New York: Norton, 1988.

Livermore, Abiel Abbot. *The Mexican War Reviewed*. 1850. Reprint. New York: Arno, 1976.

Mahan, Alfred. *The Interest of America in Sea Power: Present and Future.* Boston: Brown, Little and Co., 1897.

May, Ernest R. *Imperial Democracy: The Emergence of America as a Great Power.* New York: Harcourt, Brace and World, 1961.

McAvoy-Levy. *American Exceptionalism and US Foreign Policy.* New York: Palgrave, 2001.

Moore, John Bassett. *American Democracy.* New York, 1905.

More, Thomas. *The Complete Works of Sir Thomas More,* 4 vols. Edited by Edward Surtz and J. H. Hexter, Jr. New Haven: Yale University Press, 1965.

Morison, Samuel Eliot. *The Oxford History of the American People.* New York and Oxford: Oxford University Press, 1965.

Morrison, Samuel Eliot, and Henry Commager. *The Growth of the American Republic.* 2 vols. New York: Oxford University Press, 1950.

Marx, Leo. *The Machine in the Garden: Technology and the Pastoral Ideal in America.* London: Oxford University Press, 1964.

Masden, Deborah. *American Exceptionalism.* Edinburgh: Edinburgh University Press, 1998.

Novick, Peter. *That Noble Dream: The "Objectivity Question" and the American Historical Profession.* Cambridge: Cambridge University Press, 1988.

Orwell, George. "Notes on Nationalism." In *George Orwell: Collected Essays.* London: Martin, Secker and Warburg, 1961.

Paine, Thomas. *The Writings of Thomas Paine.* 4 vols. New York: G. P. Putnam Sons, 1894.

——— *The Complete Writings of Thomas Paine,* 2 vols. Edited by Phillip S. Foner. New York: 1945.

Parrington, Vernon L. *Main Currents in American Thought.* 3 vols. 1927. New York: Harcourt, Brace and World, Inc.; Norman, OK and London: University of Oklahoma Press, 1930.

Perkins, Dexter. *A History of the Monroe Doctrine.* 1941. Boston and Toronto: Brown and Little and Company, 1955.

Pinckney, Alphonso. *The American Way of Violence.* New York: Random House, 1971.

Potter, *People of Plenty: Economic Abundance and the American Character*, Chicago, 1954.

Poussin, Guillaume Tell. *Chemins de Fer Americains.* Paris: 1836.

——— *The United States: Its Power and Progress.* London: 1855.

Powaski, Ronald E. *Toward an Entangling Alliance: American Isolationism, Internationalism, and Europe, 1901-1950.* New York: Greenwood Press, 1991.

Pownall, Thomas. *A Memorial Most Humbly Addressed to the Sovereigns of Europe.* London: 1780.

——— *A Memorial Addressed to the Sovereigns of America.* London: 1783.

Prestowitz, Clyde. *Rogue Nation: American Unilateralism and the failure of Good Intensions*. New York: Basic Books, 2003.

Price, Glenn W. *Origins of the War with Mexico*. Austin: University of Texas Press, 1967.

Price, Richard. *Additional Observations on the Nature and Value of Civil Liberty and the War with America*. London, 1777.

——— *Observations on the Nature of Civil Liberty, the Principles of Government, and the justice and policy of the War with America*, 5th Edition. London: 1776.

——— *Observations on the Importance of the American Revolution*, 2nd Edition. London: 1785.

Ramsey, David. *An Oration in Commemoration of American Independence*. Charleston, SC: 1794.

Rapson, Richard L., ed. *Individualism and Conformity and the American Character*, Lexington, MA: D. C. Heath and Company, 1967.

Raynal, Abbé Guillaume Thomas, Franois. *The Revolution in America*. London, 1781.

Reid, T. R. *The United States of Europe: The New Superpower and the End of American Supremacy*. New York: Penguin Books, 2004.

Rhees, Morgan J. *The Good Samaritan: An Oration*. Philadelphia: 1796.

Rieselbach, Leroy N. *The Roots of Isolationism: Congressional Voting and Presidential Leadership in Foreign Policy*. Indianapolis, New York and Kansas City: The Bobbs-Merrill Company, Inc., 1966.

Rodó, José Enrique. *Ariel*. Translated by F. J. Stinson. Boston and New York: Houghton Mifflin Company, 1922.

——— *Ariel*, Translated by Margaret Sayers Paden. Austin: University of Texas Press, 1988.

Roosevelt, Theodore. *The Winning of the West*. 4 vols. 1889-1896. New York and London: G. P. Putnam's Sons, 1902-3.

——— *The Strenuous Life: Essays and Addresses*. 1900. New York: Century, 1902.

Rusk, Dean. "A Defense of American Foreign Policy." In Bliss and Johnson, *Consensus at the Crossroads*.

Schlesinger Jr., Arthur M. *The Age of Jackson*. Boston: Brown and Little, 1953.

——— "America, Experiment or Destiny?" In *American Historical Review*, 82 (1977), 505-22.

——— "The One Against the Many." In Schlesinger Jr. and Morton, *Paths of American Thought*, 531-540.

——— *Paths to the Present*. New York: Macmillan Co. 1949.

Schlesinger Jr., Arthur M. and Morton White, ed. *Paths of American Thought*. Boston: Haughton Mifflin Company, 1963.

Shafer, Byron E. ed. *Is American Different? A New Look at American Exceptionalism*. Oxford: Clarendon Press, 1991.

———— Shafer, Byron E. "What is the American Way? Four Themes in Search of Their Next Incarnation." In Scafer, *Is American Different*.

Slotkin, Richard. *Regeneration through Violence: The Mythology of the American Frontier*. Middletown, CT: Wesleyan University Press, 1973.

Smith, Anthony. *Nationalism and Modernity: A Critical Survey of Recent Theories of Nations and Nationalism*. London and New York: Routledge, 1998.

———— *Nationalism, Theory, Ideology, History*. Cambridge: Polity Press, 2001.

———— *Theories of Nationalism*. New York: Harper and Row, 1979.

Smith, Henry Nash. *The Virgin Land: The American West as Symbol and Myth*. Cambridge, MA: Harvard University Press, 1950.

Stephanson, Anders. *Manifest Destiny: American Expansionism and the Empire of Right*. New York: Hill and Wang, 1995.

Stillman, Edmund and William Pfaff, "Toward a New Foreign Policy." In Bliss and Johnson, *Consensus at the Crossroads*.

Stimson, Henry L. and McGeorge Bundy. *On Active Service in Peace and War*. New York: Harper, 1947.

Strong, Josiah. *Our Country: Its Possible Future and Its Present Crisis*. Revised Edition. 1891. Cambridge, MA, Belknap Press of the Harvard University Press, 1963.

Temin, Peter. "Free Land and Federalism: American Economic Exceptionalism." In Shafer, *Is American Different?*.

Tocqueville, Alexis de. *Democracy in America*. Edited by Phillips Bradley, New York: 1945.

Tredgold, Thomas. *The Steam Engine*, 2 vols. London: 1838.

Turner, Frederick Jackson. *The Frontier in American History*. 1920. Huntington, NY: Robert E. Krieger Company, 1976.

Twain, Mark. *Following the Equator*. 2 vols. New York: Harper Brothers, 1899.

Wachtel, Paul L. *The Poverty of Affluence: A Psychological Portrait of the American Way of Life*. Philadelphia: New Society Publishers, 1989.

Walsh, Jeffery, and James Aulich, ed. *Vietnam Images: War and Representation*. Basingstoke: Macmillan, 1989.

Weber, Max. *The Protestant Ethic and the Spirit of Capitalism*, 1905, New York: Scribner's, 1935.

Weinberg, Albert K. *Manifest Destiny: A Study of Nationalist Expansion in American History*. Baltimore: The Johns Hopkins Press, 1935.

White, Morton. *Social Thought in American: The Revolt Against Formalism*. New York, Viking, 1949.

Wildavsky, Aaron. "Resolved, that Individualism and Egalitarianism be Made Compatible in American: Political-Cultural Roots." In Shafer, *Is American Different?*.

Williams, Samuel. *A Discource on the Love of Our Country. Salem*, MA: 1775.

Williams, William Appleman, "The Rise of American World Power." In Johnson and Bliss, *Consensus at the Crossroads*.

——— *The Tragedy of American Diplomacy*. New York, Delta Books, 1962.

Winthrop, John. *The History of New England from 1630 to 1649*, 2 vols. Edited by James Savage. Boston: 1853.

Wittkopf, Eugene R. *Faces of Internationalism: Public Opinion and American Foreign Policy*. Durham, NC: Duke University Press, 1990.

Wyle, Walter E. *American World Policies*. New York: 1917.

INDEX

177

Printed in the United States
58260LVS00003B/346-348

9 780875 864679